MW00800677

Promote Wild Food Certainty
through
Plant Identification Walks

written and illustrated
by Linda Runyon

A Wild Food Company Publication

Promote Wild Food Certainty through Plant Identification Walks

February 2013

Published by the Wild Food Company

Dorchester, Massachusetts

DISCLAIMERS

This book is intended to be a tool for the establishment and identification of wild food plant exhibits for educational purposes. The information presented in this book regarding consuming wild food is for use as a supplement to a healthy, well-rounded lifestyle. The nutritional requirements of individuals may vary greatly, therefore the author and publisher take no responsibility for an individual using and ingesting wild food.

There are many variations of plants and the additional danger of poisionous look-alikes; as such, all responsibility lies with the forager. Do not rely on any one reference, but rather use several good references. The author finds this reference adequate from her experience, but you must develop your own research, observations and experience.

State and local regulations on foraging vary, but mostly there are restrictions against taking wild food from public land. You should always check with park officials before foraging anywhere but on your own land. If you know you are, or might be, on private land and wish to forage there, be sure to get the land owner's permission to do so.

Investigate and abide by all laws before building a wild food walk.

ISBN 978-0-936699-29-5

Printed in the United States of America

OfTheField.com

The Wild Food Company
101 Train Street, Suite 1
Dorchester, MA 02122

Other Wild Food Survival Materials by Linda Runyon

The Essential Wild Food Survival Guide

Wild Food Identification Guide

Linda Runyon's Master Class on Wild Food Survival DVD

Eat the Trees!

Wild Cards®

A Survival Acre

Homestead Memories

Why Not LOVE? by Ken Heitz, illustrated by Linda Runyon

Wild Food & Animals Coloring Book

Basic Middle Eastern Desert Survival Guide

DEDICATION

I dedicate this effort and research to my dear friends David Schultz, Richard Bond and his wife Stefie, and their family. These friends of mine I write about in this book treated me like an equal in all respects during the Glendale library years, as if I were a botanist and plant expert such as themselves. Working with them was a true privilege, and those years stand out in my memory as my most precious in the wild plant world. I am so grateful to the city of Glendale, Arizona, for letting David Schultz bring me on board even though I did not have the credentials for a city worker. David truly believed in the theory of wild food survival and a ready food source.

Richard Bond, a cactus expert, did most all of the physical labor intense jobs and I was privileged to work with a fine scientific mind extraordinaire. He took many gorgeous slides that documented the Glendale walk, and also kept a record of the planting and maintenance of the project throughout.

I also wish to thank Sue Henry, who, though disabled, did not let that interfere with her much appreciated research assistance, and whose contributions helped so much in the creation of this book.

There are many others who involved themselves in our efforts and they are in my debt forever. Michael Morearty, all my apprentices, and last but not least, Joan Schultz. She became a daily partner in the maintenance of this project. Their assistance with the desert challenges for this particular walk is greatly appreciated.

Lastly, I revere the memory of working with Anne LaBastille in the Adirondack mountains toward their ecology. May this book honor her passing.

TABLE OF CONTENTS

Part 1: Starting Out 1

   Chart: Properties of Wild Edible Foods 2

Part 2: The Planning Stage 9

   Separating the Exhibits 10

   Handling Weed "Wanderers" 11

   The Scope of the Walk 14

Part 3: My First Official Wild Food Walks 17

   ❧ Sabael Walk, Sabael, NY 17

   ❧ Burke's Cottages Garden, Sabael, NY 18

   ❧ Runyon Institute Walk, Warrensburg, NY 22

      Transplanting Seedlings 24

      Transplanting Wild Edibles table 25

   ❧ Rafting the Glen Walk, Warrensburg, NY 28

      Drying Wild Foods 29

   ❧ Nantikote Lenni Lenape Walk, Bridgeton, NJ 32

Part 4: The Biosphere Experiment 35

Part 5: Desert Adventures, & Ambitious Walk 37

   ❧ Hazel McManus Wild Food Walk, Sun City, AZ 39

   ❧ Glendale Library Walk, Glendale, AZ 41

      Plants and Potting 41

      The Holding Tank 42

      Holding Tank Observations 44

Preparing the Squares 45

Research Opportunities, Planting 47

The Water System, Tools 48

The Signs Project 49

Insect Control 52

Dealing with Desert Soil, Desert & other Grasses 53

The Cattail and Sunflower Exhibits 56

Arizona Master Gardeners Visit 58

Summary of General Preparation Steps for the
   Glendale Arizona Walk 62

Our Most Successful Exhibit 63

~ Tumbleweed Elementary School, Phoenix, AZ 83

Part 6: Back to the East Coast 87

~ A Natural Garden Walk, Bridgeton, NJ 87

~ Fordville Walk, Fordville, NJ 91

Holding Tank for the Fordville Walk 95

Fordville Walk Grasses 117

~ Children of the Earth Walk, Greenwich, NJ 122

Survival Backpack Kit 133

Part 7: General Tips for Wild Food Walks ... 137

Additional Data on Seedlings 137

Edible Plants and Meal Suggestions 145

Facts to Know About Wild Food Walks 150

Suggested Actions for a Successful Walk ... 152

Part 8: Presenting Wild Food to the World ... 155

PREFACE

Think of our Earth as a grid that holds the possibility of free, natural food for all of us. This grid includes valleys, hills, mountains, deserts, lakes, oceans. In most all dirt areas, plant seeds have drifted due to wind, birds, and just plain propagation. Now, countries such as the U.S., China, France, England, Turkey, Iraq, Iran and Africa, to name a few, all have the same "weeds" or natural foods. These foods grow in plain sight along paths, roadways, around rubbish, rocks, and deserted backyards. This is not complicated; indeed, it is one of the most basic of the survival gifts of nature.

It is in the interests of everyone to learn about these wild plants, and any person, group or organization that provides this data is doing a service to mankind. Survival classes, which generally include wild food plant data, are taught in military groups from the U.S. to China. Other people and groups discuss it, so why are we not using this food more often?

The ramifications of a free food source are staggering. Who would not appreciate a soup made from the wild thistle plant, or a dandelion salad with additional flavorful wild greens, or breads made from amaranth flour (to name only one of the many type of flours potentially made from "weeds")? These life-saving, essentially free meals would be especially appreciated by anyone who has ever experienced slow starvation.

Such wild food education would and can eliminate world hunger in a way that is natural and most beneficial for a body and soul. On all levels, education can and does enhance a human "way of life" and helps to provide the key point of wild food survival, which is *identification.*

Simplicity among thousands of green plants becomes the simple fact, but making the identification of a single specie is the foremost problem. If we were to use only a few of the most prevalent plants and provide clear photos, careful ID facts, cards, coloring books, and a substantial recipe book, along with a field guide and DVD, we might be able to raise the awareness of this unheralded and nutritious food supply to all.

In summary, when everyone can identify nature's vast resources of wild food, the world will have learned to eat for free, because all will have discovered that there are free wild groceries in their backyard, and "world hunger" or threats of food shortages will be relegated to the dust bins of yesteryear.

ACKNOWLEDGMENTS

Thanks to Rosary Shepherd for layout, editing and typesetting, and my son Eric for cover design and graphics handling. This wouldn't have been possible without you both! Thanks also to Holly Drake.

Linda Runyon

INTRODUCTION

On the last page of my book *Homestead Memories*, which is a collection of stories about the experiences (often hilarious, but always informative) of my life on a homestead, I wrote this about how I felt when I returned to civilization:

"In an effort to figure out who I was, really, and what I should be doing, I found my prayers being answered each time I encountered in my backyard any of the wild foods that had sustained us during those wilderness years. I realized that I had acquired a wealth of information that few in this current, frantic world ever contemplated at all.

"I had to learn quite a lot about the business end of teaching. My hard-won knowledge went to the many hundreds of people who sincerely wanted to learn the information I had to impart. In the process, I created a number of successful wild food walks, I wrote books, created a survival card deck, and continued my art work."

This book contains the details of those "wild food walks". Every walk was essentially a teaching area I created that contained a number of different wild edible plants that were brought to a central location, then planted and cultivated. Each plant had its own small plot and an identification sign. People could come from all over to walk through this exhibit of a variety of wild plants, and to increase their certainty of wild food identification, plus learn other important facts about the free food that flourishes around them. Some walks were created in a backyard and contained a few important wild plants, while others were larger in size and displayed hundreds of wild plants. The largest of my wild food walks, at the Glendale Library in Arizona, was visited by thousands of people.

I created walks with individuals, with families, with children in schools, with scouts, with communities, with survival groups, with nature groups, etc. The information gathered and included in this book would be applicable to any person or group that has access to a piece of ground. For example, such a collection of identified free food planted throughout a walkway could become a destination point for school field trips. In that way, children, parents, teachers and administrators could learn the basics of wild food survival. Visitors to a walk could return home with the decision to plant their own wild food walk in their community. This is how an idea that benefits everyone gets started and gradually becomes a sustainable way of life for all.

I can envision walks being created anywhere there are interested people who are willing to do the creative design, the implementation and upkeep of the walk, and who have as a goal to help themselves and their fellow man. And really, who would not want to learn the very basic survival skill of wild food identification? Everybody needs to eat, and this is a way that everybody can learn to eat for free from nature's bounty!

Linda Runyon
2013

Promote Wild Food Certainty through Plant Identification Walks

A wild asparagus that did not have to be stalked in the woods because it was incorporated into this early Linda Runyon wild food walk.

PART 1: Starting Out

The first thing to find out about wild plants is: Which are the ones we can eat for food? My book *The Essential Wild Food Survival Guide* lists the 60 most common edible wild plants that grow world-wide. The chart on the following page of the "Properties of Wild Edible Foods" from my Field Guide shows those common wild foods, along with important data specific to each one.

From that group I have found that the following are the most selective for planting a wild identification walk. Of course, specific areas have local edible wild plants that you could research, and additionally you could grow special plants that flourish in your particular environment.

Dandelion
Violet
Plantain, long leaf
Plantain, short leaf
Clover, red
Clover, white
Sorrel, garden
Sorrel, field
Wild lettuces
Thistles
Amaranth
Lambs Quarters
Nettles
Aloe Vera

Mints of your choice
Pine tree
Balsam tree
Maple tree
Mustards
Daisies
Purslane
Shepherd's purse
Cattail dried exhibit
Day lilies
Crabgrasses
Barnyard grass
Phragmities
Milkweed

Properties Of Wild Edible Foods

Plant	Annual	Biennial	Perennial	Native to N.A.	Naturalized	Harvest Time	Leaves/needles	Stems	Buds	Flowers/Catkins	Fruit	Seeds	Roots	Freezes	Dries	Vegetable/Fruit	Herb	Tea	Flour	Field Guide Page
Aloe Vera					●	Spring/Summer	●	●	●	●				●		●	●	●		52
Amaranth				●		Summer	●	●		●		●		●	●	●			●	54
Arrowhead			●	●		Fall		●					●	●	●	●				55
Aster			●	●		Fall	●	●	●	●		●	●	●	●	●		●	57
Balsam Fir				●		Year-round	●	●	●	●		●			●	●	●	●	●	58
Birch				●		Year-round		●	●	●		●		●	●	●	●	●	●	60
Blackberry				●		Year-round		●			●	●		●	●	●				62
Blueberry				●		Summer	●				●	●		●	●	●		●		64
Bulrush			●			Summer/Fall		●	●	●		●	●	●	●	●	●	●	●	65
Burdock		●				Year-round	●	●	●	●		●	●	●	●	●	●	●	●	67
Cattail			●	●		Year-round	●	●	●	●		●	●	●	●	●	●	●	●	69
Chamomile	●				●	Spring/Summer	●	●		●		●		●	●	●	●	●	●	72
Chickweed	●				●	Year-round	●	●	●	●		●		●	●	●	●	●	●	73
Chicory			●		●	Spring	●	●		●	●		●	●	●	●	●	●		75
Cholla			●			May			●		●	●	●	●	●	●			●	76
Clover			●		●	Year-round	●	●	●	●		●	●	●	●	●		●	●	78
Crabgrass			●		●	Year-round		●				●		●	●	●			●	80
Daisy			●		●	Year-round	●	●	●	●		●		●	●	●	●	●	●	81
Dandelion			●		●	Year-round	●	●	●	●			●	●	●	●	●	●	●	83
Dock			●			Spring/Fall	●	●		●		●	●	●	●	●	●	●	●	85
Evening Primrose		●		●		Summer/Fall						●	●	●	●	●				86
Filarie		●				Winter/Spring									●	●				87
Fireweed			●	●		Spring/Summer	●	●	●	●		●	●	●	●	●	●	●	●	89
Goldenrod			●	●		Spring/Sum/Fall	●	●	●	●		●	●	●	●	●	●	●	●	90
Grape			●	●		Fall	●	●	●	●	●	●	●	●	●	●	●	●	●	92

2

Plant	Season	Page
Lamb's Quarters	Summer/Fall	93
Malva	Winter/Spring	95
Maple	Summer	97
Meadowsweet	Summer	98
Milk Thistle	Spring/Summer	99
Milkweed	Spring/Sum/Fall	101
Mint	Spring/Fall	103
Mullein	Spring/Fall	105
Mustard	Spring	107
Nettles	Spring/Fall	108
Phragmities	Summer	109
Pine	Year-round	110
Plantain	Year-round	111
Prickly Pear	Summer	113
Purslane	Summer	115
Queen Anne's Lace	Summer	116
Raspberry	Summer	117
Rose	Spring/Fall	118
Saguaro	Summer	120
Sheep (Garden) Sorrel	Spring/Summer	121
Shepherd's Purse	Summer	122
Sow Thistle	Winter/Spring	124
Strawberry	Spring	125
Sumac	Summer	126
Sunflower	Spring/Summer	127
Thistle	Spring/Fall	128
Thyme	Summer/Fall	129
Tumbleweed	Spring/Summer	131
Violet	Spring/Summer	132
Wild Lettuce	Spring/Summer	133
Willow	Year-round	134
Wintergreen	Spring/Summer	135
Wood Sorrel	Spring/Fall	137
Yarrow	Spring/Fall	138

Wild food walks can come in all sizes, shapes and varieties. The very first walk I ever did was more of a discovery process for me. I was curious and wanted to find out how many edible wild plants would come up in a tilled area of ground 3 feet by 3 feet. (Hint: A rototiller can be used to get up anything already growing there, so you are left with just soil.) I had some wonderful hours stringing out that 3 foot by 3 foot square of my yard. I found out that if your lawn is lush, the wild plants that come up will be lush too, and that whatever soil sustains beautiful grass also has beautiful weeds. I do prefer the lush lawn weeds, small as they are, because they are tough and more than ready to shoot up from the cutting lawnmower.

After I had staked out my plot, I kept an eye on it and actually took a stool and studied every square inch of grass. I found over 7 wild plants, and a few different types of grasses. On inspection, you will see these same plants, give or take a few, in most grassy areas, including in the city. An outstanding discovery, as I thought, "How lucky I was to find 7 different types of foods in my staked-out yard." The sum of all this abundance showed me so many ways to show others.

With all of this wild food growing in my small plot, I got the idea to dry them and try to make a little identification book. Scissors are a useful tool for cutting off leaves of the dandelion, plantain, clover, red and white, chamomile, sorrel. After I picked individual plants and the leaves had dried thoroughly, I pressed them onto clear contact paper. I cut 4-inch sections around them, keyhole-punched them, and strung them together to create my unique identification booklet! I gave away hundreds over the following year.

4

Eventually, this little starter booklet grew into one that included miniature leaves of clover, dandelion, wild lettuce, plantain, chamomile, strawberry, yarrow, thyme, and others, so that I would have a consistent identification pack for the students that I began to teach in significant numbers; I often created fifty student identification packs. For the novice enthusiast, these became an integral part of learning the skills of a forager. And, of course, those little kits were the precursor to my very popular "Wild Food Card Deck".

Another very interesting result from my little plot of those 7 plants that I picked over and over (and froze to accumulate a quantity of food), was that some apprentices and I were able to put on a dinner for 200 people from only a few feet of lawn. We served six courses, and still the guests came back for more. It was quite a rewarding (and tasty!) experience for all involved.

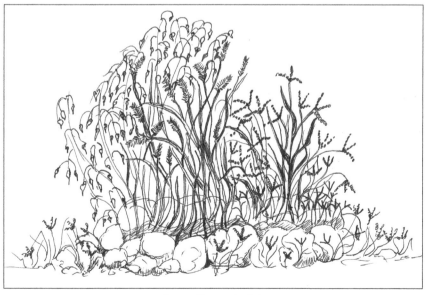

A small weed plot.

One of the other smaller walks that I did, and which I remember fondly, was with a marvelous woman and her three children. They made a game out of building a wild food plot in their back yard. The two teens took my deck of Wild Cards and picked out 10 plants each. The youngest child, a 7-year old, enjoyed putting single marking sticks every 2 feet into the rototilled dirt. He also did a wonderful job of stringing in between the sticks to mark out the boundary of the plot.

Once the two teens had decided on their plants, we three took a brief walk so they could familiarize themselves with the backyard species as I identified them. Each teen was given a trowel, spoon, pail and shallow box. I encouraged them to dig at least 5 or 6 of the individual species for planting, plus maybe a plant in flower, or several in different stages of growth. One teen collected 6 red clovers, 6 white clovers, 6 dandelions, 6 daisies, and so on. The other student found 6 of both types of plantain, 6 shepherd's purse, etc.

Basic items for a simple yard walk.

The samples were transplanted to the tilled plot and identified using popsicle sticks and a marking pencil. The planting had begun, as had a wonderful lesson in fun and survival for the whole family.

I followed these same basic procedures with many families and students over the years on their private lawns, backyards, and wooded areas.

A little walk I put in where I lived in later years.

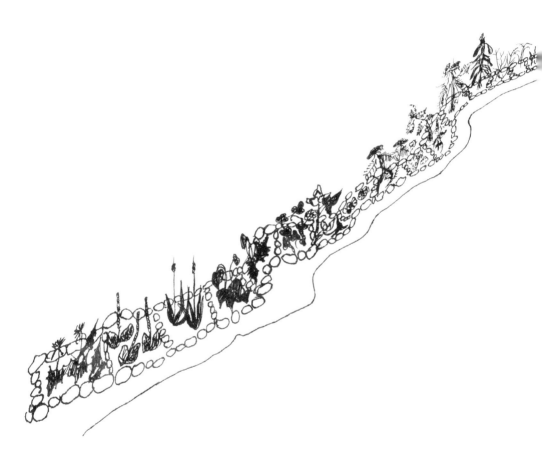

PART 2: The Planning Stage

The Blueprint

Over the years I learned by trial and error (naturally) how to plan and carefully place the various plants that I would include in any proposed walk. I started with the overall dimensions allowed for the walk, and drew out a plan on paper. This became my blueprint for the walk, and after a while I would get a feel for how many of what kind of plant would be the most useful and informative for the visitors that might come to learn from that walk. I always made sure to include plants local to the area, along with as many of the common wild plants as I could successfully grow in the exhibit. I found some stencils that helped me design my plan, and here's a sample of one of them.

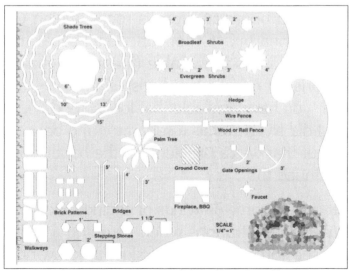

Many type of stencils are available.

As I created each new walk, I learned more about the kinds of different tools, equipment, water sources, potting supplies, soil additives, exhibit markers and signs, brochures, etc., that went into creating a success-ful and sought-after wild food walk. After each one, I knew to include more data in the planning process for the next walk.

I also learned that it's a good idea to consult with local Master Gardener clubs for any specific details on weather, soil, etc., as part of the planning stage because it could help avoid surprises later on!

Separating the Exhibits

One of the more important actions of planning and instituting a walk is making sure that each plant is clearly separate from its neighbor. Weeds especially have a tendency to grow anywhere, and it became a game for me to work out methods of keeping the various plants separated from each other so people could easily identify their features. A useful and handy separator and boundary item is rocks, which you can usually find nearby. Other functional separators are bricks, railroad ties if available (these also make good foundations for raised plant beds), shingles — basically whatever you have available that looks good and will do the job. I did try gravel as a separator and boundary for a walk, but that was a problem for the handicapped, so I discontinued that.

Here are some drawings of edgings and separators that I used as illustrations when planning a walk. You will also see some of them in follow-up drawings that I did of my walks.

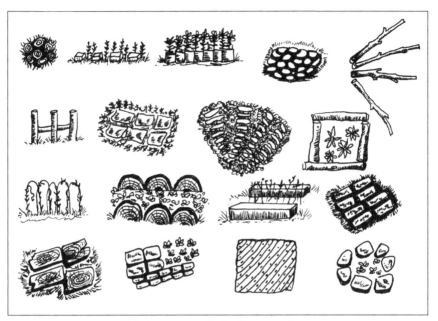

Edgings and Path Decorations

Top (left to right): crosscut circular slices of log, bricks, 2 by 4 ends buried in ground, smooth egg-shaped rocks with soil in between, straight limbs or poles.

Second row (left to right): Natural fences from wood, larger slate pieces, roundish stones, cut poles in a raised bed.

Third row (left to right): Cross fencing or picket sections, crosscut logs halved, 2 by 4's.

Bottom row (left to right): large cut lumber boards, flagstones or bricks, decking or patio lumber, stones.

Handling Weed "Wanderers"

It took me a while, but I finally did develop a particularly effective method of keeping the plants I called "wanderers" separated from one another. The main wanderers to watch for are: nettles, mints, aloe, most grasses (especially crab grasses), milkweed and garden sorrel. Tendrils, tubers, and shoots can wander underground for many inches, even many feet. Any

11

openings are access for the wanderers to come out and come up to the surface to propagate.

Early on I put gravel over the visitor walking areas, but found wheelchairs could not go over the it. I would now suggest some sort of path next to the exhibit. Sometimes we rolled black mulch over the black paper and that worked fairly well. At least the wheelchair could go with someone pushing it fairly smoothly. Hard dirt is the best for the walk-around path, but of course cement or wood would be the prime way to do the walk.

Here's how to effectively keep wandering plants separated:

Dig a square or rectangle pit the dimensions of your plot for the plant and save the dirt on the side.

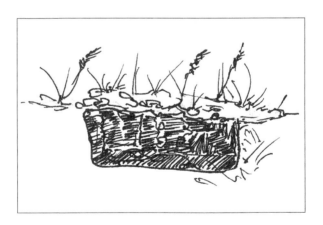

Put one section of cloth, or screening, or black paper (you could even use sections of sheet metal), in and over the sides and bottom of the pit. I used black paper or black cloth to keep out the weeds. (I have met folks that used tent pegs to keep the cloth stable under the gravel. If you do that, be sure to cover thoroughly so the pegs do not trip people up.) The one exception to this might be sheet metal for the nettles. After many walks, I finally learned to use sheet metal with any prolific plant that will go through any crack or hole in your separator method. Sheet metal cut to size worked finally, using the black cloth first, then the sheet metal

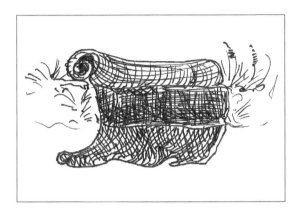

sections. After this, fill the dirt back in.

<u>Always</u> place the wanderers apart from each other. Putting a tree in between allows you to group rocks, pebbles, or gravel, and makes it easier for the maintenance person to spot the wanderers popping up where they shouldn't.

The Scope of the Walk

An essential part of your planning is to have some idea of how big or small you want the completed walk to be, and how long you want it to continue as a functioning walk. If you are putting one in your back yard and plan for it to mostly be developed and tended by your family and friends, then the planning stage is fairly straightforward. Decide which wild plants you want to have (or let them show themselves to you on a cultivated piece of ground), separate them, identify them on a card, and make sure they get enough water. Harvest them as needed, and enjoy the free bounty.

At the other end of the scale is a walk that you would like to see be viable for many years and experienced by many people. A walk of this magnitude, though, will require a significant outlay of time and energy (and probably some money) even after it is set up and doing well. If it is a community endeavor, you will likely need permits and there may be additional legal steps to take. And for sure you will need a lot of help. There is routine upkeep, watering, transplanting, harvesting, weeding, etc., that must be done to keep the area in a condition to be seen by the public, and especially if an entrance fee is requested. Be sure to include these details in your planning, along with any printing expenditures for things like hand-outs, brochures (I have included a sample later in this book), schedules, books, DVDs on wild food, etc.

One time I was asked to do a walk for the blind on the west coast. After the safety costs and ease for the disabled were estimated, the project was scraped. So be sure that you gather all the data possible for your walk during the planning stage. As to that proposed walk for the blind, it's too bad. I do envision a wonderful walk for blind people where questions in the exhibit are asked in Braille, and they are asked to pick certain plains in the exhibit, to feel them and discover the texture and leaf shape, and smell them. It would be great to include all mints in such as walk, as there are dozens of them plus other aromatic plants safe to pick, smell, and taste-test. This walk could also include prickerless roses, and shasta daisy, whose leaves are just delicious to eat raw.

The main point about the planning stage is to 1) decide what it is you would like for people to take away from their visit to your walk, 2) combine that with what you and your fellow walk builders can realistically do, and then 3) do your best to provide that. The data in this book should be enough to help you with the actions, items and details to build a successful walk, of whatever size or scope.

A depiction of a natural garden and surrounding wild food as diagrammed in my first book, *A Survival Acre*

PART 3: My First Official Wild Food Walks

Sabael Walk, 1982-1983
Sabael, New York

I had spent so many years sustaining myself and my family with wild food that it was second nature to me to apply what I had learned to create a wild food area on my first property after leaving the wilderness. This was in Sabael, NY. I loved this first public walk around my cottage where I had electricity for the first time in 13 years.

This location contained a variety of the wild plants I knew would be important for people to accurately identify when they encountered them in their foraging trips. I knew that I wanted to call the exhibit a "Wild Food Walk", because people would come and walk through a specially cultivated and tended area that displayed many different edible plants for them to view, identify, and learn about.

Drawing on prior experience in cultivating wild plants, I realized that to get best results for this particular walk, I would need to have raised beds (for which I used non-creosote-covered railroad ties) and added topsoil. I placed rocks around the natural areas and built bridges over the swamp that was on the property, and that was the layout of my first walk. The opposite page shows my diagram of that first walk.

17

You can make up your own symbols for the various items in your walks, but you probably will want to be consistent with the symbols from one diagram to the next.

Of course, I always kept and used wild food that was removed from any walk exhibit I created, because all of it was edible and nutritious. During the first winter after I built this first walk, I used heavy hay to protect my plants. Another thing I learned for this walk is that peat moss may help keep the surrounding weeds from inundating your food strip.

The second year of the walk all of the species showed regrowth except for a sparse wintergreen patch. Unfortunately, the presence of red dots on leaves indicated an over-acidic soil due to nearby balsam trees, which were natural to the area. All plant beds were peat mossed for the second summer.

This walk was seen by over 3000 people whom I toured personally. After that summer I was fortunate that down the street from me lived Rose and Bruce Burke, who were able to give me an area of land so I could create my second wild food walk. The plants in the first walk at my cottage were naturally incorporated back into the lawn.

Burke's Cottages Garden, 1983-1985
Sabael, New York

Here is the summary of this second walk that I created, and in which I gave a tour twice daily for two summers, though the walk itself was kept up for three years.

18

First Year: Rototilled a strip of lawn and transferred plants I found to rock-ringed sections. Added 6 inches of peat moss after one month's growth. Some harvesting and thinning were necessary.

Second Year: Regrowth was fantastic—100%.

Third Year: Good regrowth in most beds; poor regrowth of grape, meadowsweet, cattail (unattended).

Fourth Year: Plants assimilated back into mowed lawn.

(Note: In this walk I had a mullein plant that grew to 10 feet tall.)

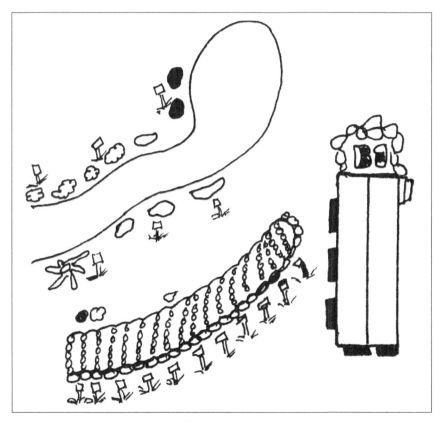

Diagram for the Burke's Cottage garden walk

19

The welcoming sign at Burke's Cottages walk

A rototilled walk easily done and maintained.
Note the two mullein in the middle, 3 feet tall already.

A Survival Acre

50 Northeastern
Wild Foods & Medicines

Survival Acre

Linda Runyon is an expert on such foods. She became one out of interest and out of necessity. She came here from New Jersey with her son Todd

The necessity of stretching food dollars and interest sparked by the necessity have resulted in the establishment of Survival Acre, where Linda now offers wild food seminars.

Not only is food gathering fun and inexpensive, it is also healthier. For example, a cup of rosehip tea could provide nearly enough vitamin C for an average person. And for those on special diets, did you know that Queen Anne's lace, a plant growing abundantly in Adirondack fields and on Adirondack lawns, can be used as a salt substitute? Instead of sugar laden soft drink, serve your children a chilled spearmint or wintergreen tea.

Although many of the foods have been consumed by Adirondack families for years (surprising how many people eat milkweed!), the value of Linda's seminars is not just learning what you CAN eat but also what you CANNOT eat. An uninitiated person should not go pull grass and eat it, as many wild plants are toxic. But with proper education, plants that would normally go untouched or even eliminated from our lawn can provide a delicious and nutritious addition to family menus. Just ask Linda!

Call for a PRIVATE appointment for your family

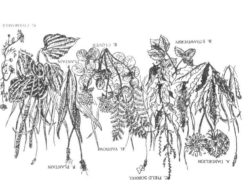

D. BURDOCK
E. CLOVER
P. PLANTAIN
B. STRAWBERRY
D. YARROW
C. FIELD SORREL
A. DANDELION

Wild Food
A Healthy, Tasty Alternative

LINDA RUNYON

- Wild food expert, author and forager
- Registered nurse
- Grandmother
- 12 yr. homestead experience
- Use of Iroquois methods
- Diet: *entirely wild foods*

LECTURES
  TOURS
    SLIDES
      RESOURCE MATERIAL
        BOOK: *A Survival Acre*
        RECIPE BOOK: *Groceries in the Backyard*

Located at Burke's Cottages, Lake shore Drive, Sabael, New York. Located four (4) miles up route 30 from the Town of Indian Lake. Lakeshore Drive to the left and ¼ mile down. Lodging is available. Contact at 518-281-4983 or 518-648-5151.

Public tours are $3.00 each and children under 10 years are FREE.

Monday, Tuesday   9 am-10 am
Thursday and Friday   3 pm- 4 pm
   4 pm- 5 pm

Lectures and slides are also shown at the Indian Lake American Legion Hall on most Wednesday nights as posted. Lectures are scheduled from 7 pm-9 pm.

Plan some time at SURVIVAL ACRE

Here is a flyer that I put together to advertise the walk at Burke's Cottages. It was a successful way to get the word out not only about the walk, but to also let people know that I was doing lectures at a local hall and that they could come there to find out about wild food. There are always many ways to promote a walk so that people can come and learn about wild food. We didn't have the internet when I did my walks, but I can imagine it would be a great promotion tool.

Runyon Institute Walk, 1986

Warrensburg, New York

The Runyon Institute was founded by a business-man named Walter Johnson. The building was founded in my name, and I was very happy to be able to make a more careful wild food walk. This one hosted over 6,000 people who walked its paths and saw our wild food exhibit. This was the third food identification walk developed for public use and it was phenomenal. The emphasis here was to demonstrate the area's natural habitat and to show common edible lawn plants. The wild food from the walk provided food for 12 staff, myself, and guests.

Days were kept busy gathering, cooking, and studying, as well as harvesting, drying, freezing, press-ing dried plants to make identification booklets, and helping the public. The teepee shown here was our drying rack.

The teepee at the Runyon Institute walk

The tours were conducted outside on the walk, then to the teepee to observe our gathering and drying techniques, and on into the Institute itself. There, we had a "root" room filled with woods and field roots, properly labeled, strung from nails on the wall.

Note: When you have a knowledge or education room, it encourages students to bring what they have found to that area and acquire more data. And with that room available you can take up hours of education if the walk outside was rained out. I think if you build a large identification walk, you should have a study area somewhere nearby where people can go to learn more. And of course, the sale of informative books, cards, coloring books, and DVDs, while greatly benefiting the aspiring forager, are also a financial help to your enterprise.

We had a program and a brochure for this walk that we handed out to the visitors.

I cannot imagine how productive such an institute would be today. Maintenance is essential, though. Set up is easy, building the walk is simple, but the long-time maintenance is the key to long-time success. Volunteers are imperative!

First Year: Rototilled the strip of lawn. Added topsoil, gravel walk ways, wood 2x4's in between plants transplanted from natural areas, which exhibited rapid growth. Peat moss added on successive harvesting of most sections. No fertilizers used. Plants were assimilated into lawn after first year. Unfortunately, I needed to close the institute and move closer to home in North Creek, and that's where my next walk, the white water rafting walks, began.

Runyon Institute Walk diagram

Transplanting Seedlings

At this point I want to briefly discuss transplanting seedlings, because that was something I did to get this next walk started. After a number of attempts I learned the most efficient way to successfully transplant seedlings, and here it is:

1. Take a teaspoon and dig down a "plug" of dirt to the depth of 1 full teaspoon. (Of course, if your seedlings have longer roots, use a tablespoon.)

2. Wet your new potting area until damp all over (caution: not too wet!). Using your tablespoon tool, press down areas to accept seedlings. These pre-dug areas should be deep enough for the roots of the new seedlings, and spaced apart according to type of plant.

24

Transplanting Wild Edibles

Plant Name	Planting Depth	Method	Ease of Adjustment
Aloe Vera	deep	trowel	perky
Amaranth	shallow	spoon	wilts
Aster	medium	trowel	wilts
Balsam fir	deep	shovel	perky
Birch	deep	shovel	wilts
Blackberry	deep	shovel	perky
Blueberry	deep	shovel	perky
Bulrush	deep	shovel	perky
Burdock	deep	shovel	wilts
Cattail	deep	saw, shovel	perky
Chamomile	shallow	spoon	perky
Chickweed	shallow	spoon	perky
Chicory	deep	shovel	wilts
Cholla	medium deep	shovel	perky
Clover	shallow	spoon	perky
Daisy	medium	trowel	perky
Dandelion	medium	trowel	wilts
Dock	deep	shovel	wilts
Evening Primrose	medium	shovel	perky
Field thistle	medium	spoon	wilts
Fireweed	medium	trowel	wilts
Goldenrod	deep	shovel	perky
Grape	deep	shovel	wilts
Lamb's quarters	shallow	spoon	wilts
Mallow (Malva)	medium	trowel	wilts
Maple	deep	shovel	perky
Meadowsweet	deep	shovel	perky
Milk thistle	deep	shovel	perky
Milkweed	medium deep	trowel	wilts
Mint	shallow	spoon	wilts
Mullein	deep	shovel	wilts
Mustard	medium	trowel	wilts
Nettles	deep	shovel	perky
Phragmities	deep	shovel	wilts
Pine	deep	shovel	perky
Plantain	shallow	spoon	wilts
Prickly pear	deep	shovel	perky
Rose	deep	shovel	perky
Sheep sorrel	shallow	spoon	perky
Shepherd's Purse	shallow	spoon	perky

Transplanting Wild Edibles

(continued)

Plant Name	Planting Depth	Method	Ease of Adjustment
Sow Thistle	deep	shovel	wilts
Strawberry	shallow	spoon	perky
Sumac	deep	shovel	perky
Sunflower	medium	shovel	wilts
Thyme	shallow	spoon	perky
Tumbleweed	shallow	trowel	perky
Violets	shallow	spoon	perky
Wild lettuce	medium	trowel	wilts
Willow	deep	saw, shovel	perky
Wintergreen	shallow	spoon	perky
Wood sorrel	shallow	spoon	perky
Yarrow	medium	trowel	perky

The seedlings that will need to be spaced further apart because they can grow tall and need more growing space are: wild lettuce, mullein, goldenrod, curly dock. (Hint: If the plant grows into a bush-like form, re-pot its seedlings into separate pots that you can then individuallly place in its exhibit plot. You want a single plant that is easily identifiable to people walking by, not a tightly formed bush!)

Planting 6" apart.

A bigger pot for planting 12" apart.

Something else to plan for is the height the plants will reach when fully grown. You don't want to place a plant that will grow tall in front of a short one because then the short one probably won't get enough sunlight. Here are the average heights for these full grown plants:

Short, 12" or under:

Dandelion	Wild strawberry
White Clover	Alfalfa
Garden sorrel	Chamomile
Purslane	Peppergrass
Violets	Shepherd's purse
Daisies	Yarrow
Plantains	Thyme
Chickweed	Filaree

Large, 13" or more:

Sunflower	Chicory
Amaranth	Curly dock
Lamb's quarters	Burdock
Thistles	Prickly lettuce
Primrose	Blue lettuce
Sow thistle	Malva
Cattail	Mustard

Trees and bushes, 2-3 feet to 20 feet or more:

Pine tree	Meadowsweet bush
Balsam tree	

Your new seedling growing area should be watered twice daily with a sprinkle nozzle. I never flood the area with a large stream of water. Soil should be wetted, not soaked. Remember, in the wild, sometimes the seedlings do not get rain even every day, so if you forget to water, it is not a major mistake. In fact, once in a while, I only water once a day, or not at all. I believe this toughens the plant. However, if the plants are in direct sun and the soil gets dry, you might have to water them possibly twice a day, morning and after dinner, to be sure the soil doesn't get too dry. Chapter 7 has more data and photos on transplanting seedlings.

"Rafting the Glen" Walk, 1986

Warrensburg, New York

This is a walk that I put in at Warrensburg, NY, near a white water rafting company.

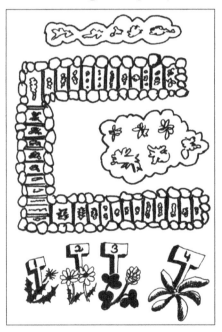

"Rafting the Glen" Walk diagram

Many of my students were young campers from that rafting company. I particularly enjoyed the river that flowed just a few yards away. The time taken to prepare and plant this walk was less than 4 hours. Placed near the Hudson River, water was never a problem and I never had to carry one bucket of water the whole time.

First Year: Put peat moss 6 inches thick around transplanted seedlings. Natural watering. Occasionally harvested smaller "lawn foods". No fertilizers added. Some trimming was done on raspberry, blackberry and roses.

Second Year: Unattended except to weed patches, add 6 inches more peat moss. All plants survived winter except for birch, pine, and cattails. Replanted more lamb's quarters.

Drying Wild Foods

I want to insert here data about homemade screens and drying wild foods. The process of drying wild food properly for storage has been addressed in my other materials, particularly *The Essential Wild Food Survival Guide*, but it deserves another mention here because you will harvest plenty of food from any wild food walk. It's unavoidable if you want to maintain a nice-looking exhibit of easily identifiable plants. As mentioned, they do grow like weeds and will overrun their designated plot, and the entire exhibit, if not properly, well, weeded.

Daily maintenance of a walk of any size could fill an entire winter's larder for several people, and I tell you that from personal experience with these walks.

Flat Rock Road, Lake George, NY, drying area

My rustic put-together was just pieces of wood framed and screened. There is a perfect drying rack pattern included in my collection of wild food materials, "The Whole Enchilada", or WEP, as found on the product page of our website, OfTheField.com.

30

Homemade drying racks

A simple drying area in a screened in porch was always filled with greens, foods and medicines. This larder increased to many gallon jars over the summer and a whole year's wild teas were added. The larder provided around 60% of my diet over those years.

Nantikote Lenni Lenape Walk, 1987-1988

Bridgeton, New Jersey

I was asked to do a wild food walk in Bridgeton City Park, on Native American land. I was pleased to work with Jim Ridgeway as well as other members of the Nantikote Lenni Lenape tribe. Research done here has been invaluable for developing future food walks. This walk was graciously maintained for 2 years by the Nantikote Lenni Lenape Indian people. Some very famous people took these walks, such as the King and Queen of Sweden, who did an in-depth tour in 1987. This walk closed in 1988.

First Year: Rototilled a strip of lawn in Bridgeton City Park. Added garden topsoil. Tepee wood stays used for wheel design and plant separation. Applied 6 inches of peat moss after 2 to 3 weeks growth.

Second Year: Unattended garden prolific with growth. Largest leaf and seeding growth of all walks. I couldn't attend this one personally but once every two months. This walk was assimilated back into the City Park park after the third year.

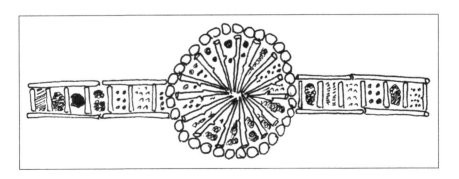

Nantikote Lenni Lenape Walk diagram

Lantikote Lenni Lenape Walk list of plants in the large "wheel" area of the walk:

dandelion	thyme
clovers, red and white	mints
strawberries	plantain
yarrow	purslane
chickweed	primrose
mustard	curly dock
violets	chamomile

"Ladder" extensions off the wheel, right and left:

maple tree	blueberry
pine tree	mullein
balsam tree	prickly pear
aloe vera	lamb's quarters
Queen Anne's lace	amaranth
raspberry	sumac
blackberry	

In 1989, *People* magazine came and did an article about me and here is an excerpt: "An expert on weeds and other wild foods, and a strict vegetarian—'an environmentarian', she calls herself—Runyon's mission is to teach people that nutritious edibles are springing up all around us free for the picking. With common weeds as the mainstay of one's diet, Runyon claims, it is entirely possible to reduce the monthly grocery bill to about $30 per person. Her greatest triumph in transforming weeds into food occurred several years ago. "I fed 200 people off 10 square feet of grass," Runyon recalls. "I spent 10 or 15 minutes on the lawn every day, and in about three weeks I had enough weeds to rent the town hall at Indian Lake, N.Y., and serve 200 dinners."

1990 magazine cover of Biosphere II.

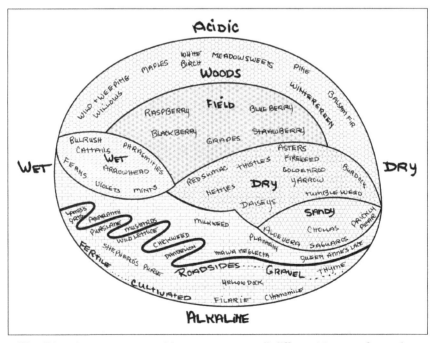

The Biosphere was meant to encompass all different types of growing environments.

PART 4: The Biosphere Experiment

Biosphere II Years 1989-1993

The Background Story of the Biosphere II Environmental Experiment

You may have heard of this experiment that was first constructed between 1987 and 1991 in Arizona. Per Wikipedia, "Biosphere II is an Earth systems science research facility currently owned by the University of Arizona since 2011. Its mission is to serve as a center for research, outreach, teaching and learning about Earth, its living systems, and its place in the universe. It is a 3.14-acre structure originally built to be an artificial, materially closed ecological system in Oracle, Arizona (US) by Space Biosphere Ventures. . . . It was used to explore the complex web of interactions within life systems in a structure that included five areas based on biomes and an agricultural area and human living/working space to study the interactions between humans, farming and technology with the rest of nature."

I had by this time moved to Arizona, and when I was asked to come and lecture about wild foods to the people who were building the Biosphere, to the staff affiliated with the project, and to the scientists who were the basis for the experiment, I was thrilled. I realized that my homestead years were even more important than I thought. I brought *A Survival Acre* and Wild Cards with me when I went to meet with the Biosphere people. My main goal was to prove that a diet of wild foods could be beneficial to the people participating in the experiment in that airtight world.

There were hundreds of wild plants in the greenhouse and I know we were a little short of 1/2 way through my identification of them when a scientist said to me, "That's enough, you know your plants." The truth is, I had never seen the world-wide handpicked plants, but I was able to operate on instinct and inherent skill from eating wild for so many years, and so I was right on target with my data. I knew which plants were best suited for tea, or food, and which could be ground into a hearty flour. I also applied my Foraging Rules for additional certainty during that "test" of my knowledge.

Later on I found it very interesting that a scientist's recommendation to folks was to eat amaranth, and it is my understanding that the Biospherians ate mainly from the Hopi red amaranth as a vegetable, which is a quick-growing and highly nutritious plant. For me personally, amaranth has been one of my daily and now weekly supplements, and I have substituted it regularly for a common vegetable portion.

My entire Biosphere II involvement was quite an acknowledgment of the value of my wild food information, and this experience had a lot to do with fueling my desire to continue to share what I knew with everybody I could reach. In fact, I did a lot of learning and teaching of desert plants during my stay in Arizona. I did some smaller walks while there, and I also was able to create my most important and impressive walk while I lived in Arizona with a lot of help.

PART 5: Desert Adventures, and My Most Ambitious Walk

By the late 1980s I had moved to Arizona and begun to learn about the edible wild desert foods available there. And of course, I shared what I learned with others who also wanted to know. I was able to teach many of my foraging and prepartion classes outside on the desert itself.

In the photo below I am demonstrating that jumping cholla can be barbecued to remove the needles. The inside edible gel of the plant is easily removed when you can handle the cholla without the sharp needles. It is not necessary to cook it, just remove the needles by burning them off.

Desert barbeque.

My friend Althea Dixon brushes the red hairs off the Nopolito cactus pads.

The stinging irritation from a single cactus hair is the reason cleaning Nopolito cactus is a necessity. Some people use rocks, some the scraping from the back of a knife. Others use course paint brushes or a scrub brush. Then the pad can be handled easily, skinned, and cut in many tiny pieces which can used as stir fry, salad, casseroles, corn bread, or my favorite, cactus salsa.

Teaching a desert class

During my years in Arizona, I also experimented with indoor wild plants. In air conditioned rooms I grew salad ingredients that were harvested from plants grown indoors in pots and baskets.

Glendale, Arizona apartment

When I first arrived in the bare desert in midsummer, the average temperature was 100 degrees. In order to get some plant growth outdoors I tried water poured in the same place, over and over, just to see one thing sprouted, but . . . nothing! So, bringing in small weeds (wild food) into pots containing potting soil was the only answer. A sunny window, not directly under the air vents and voila—salad. Apartment wild living!

Hazel McManus Wild Food Walk, 1990

Sun City, Arizona

A gourmet cook, Hazel of Sun City, Arizona, had a wild food walk in her back yard and she hosted many wild food luncheons for me, which our local television stations covered.

39

McManus Walk diagram

The scalloped lines drawn in the diagram that edge the walk were steel crochet hoops that were appropriate for this little walk. That soil was extremely caliche and like concrete, so when water was poured for several minutes, the soil became mud.

First Year: Soil prepared to deal with caliche (desert soil). Added in equal quantities peat moss, compost, topsoil. Used raised beds, wood sides. Plants easily transplanted with spoon and trowel. Irrigated with a water bubbler and hose twice a month, otherwise unattended.

Second Year: Unattended; temperatures of 110 degrees

This edible centerpiece was a beautiful product
of Hazel's backyard wild food walk.

40

for two months. Harvested remaining plants, seedlings, and seeds. This strip was assimilated back to nature.

We had aloe vera flowers on toothpicks, which are delicious dipped in sour cream! Milk thistle made the most delicious, velvety soup. Calendula petals are beautiful in a sow thistle salad. Rose petal sorbet finished this incredible meal from our walk. The Phoenix television crews were present at this one.

Glendale Library Wild Food Identification Walk, 1995-1997 (My Most Ambitious Walk)

Glendale, AZ

The walk I did at the Glendale Library was the largest and most complex of any that I did. David Schultz, water conservationist, was instrumental in the planning and maintenance of this walk and worked along with me. The following are the preparation steps we did before the walk opened to the public.

Plants and Potting

A preliminary, enjoyable task with this walk was finding native indigenous desert plants. A short hour on the desert showed us several of the plants we needed. I went out each time planning to get only one plant and ended up returning with many different types of transplants that we added to the walk eventually. Additionally, I actually bought from a nursery several plants not found on natural desert soil, namely thyme, yarrow, violets, and daisy, for display purposes.

Since I knew I would also need plenty of pots, I visited nurseries and asked for donations of black plastic pots of all sizes. I also got good potting soil that was free of bacteria or disease. Some plants were already established transplants, others were grown from seeds. I separated the established growth from the seed pots, and each was marked (using a tongue depressor) with the name of the plant and the date of its planting.

The Holding Tank

I had to have a place to keep the plants where they could survive well as we prepared the ground where they would be planted in the walk. This area I

Holding tank for the Glendale Library Walk

named the "holding tank" area. Any such area must have access to a hose or water from a reliable source so the plants can be watered regularly.

Each time I entered the outdoor area, I was aware of many cars going in and out nearby. By the time we were ready to actually construct the walk, several thousand people already knew we grew our own plants and had brought many from the desert. People would wave and toot their horns when we brought in a new plant poking out from the car rear window.

The water from the hoses was so hot when we began our daily watering that we had to use gloves to hold the hose, and let the water run for some time to obtain cool water. I found if I bunched the holding pots together in groups, they both shaded each other and seemed to grow better. I actually had to park them if they were growing too fast, as it was hard to see where to water with the hose.

Certain wild plants are very aggressive in a pot of dirt. Thistles, wild lettuce, violets, mints are but few that just explode in greenery when watered regularly and kept partially shaded in 105 degrees. Some plants took much pruning to encourage them to branch out and bush. I learned, and worried about the future, of certain plants. If they took a lot of work in the pot, I knew the exhibit would most certainly be a lot of cutting and care. They were! I highly recommend, before you open the walk to the public, that you cultivate a group of volunteers who will be willing to do those kinds of jobs. That is a must!

Here is a list of western plants that were added to this walk. Whole specimens were coaxed to grow in the holding tank and replanted.

alfalfa	tumbleweed
amaranth, Palmer	ephedra
amaranth, Hopi	filaree
aster	milk thistle
black mustard	prickly pear
chia	saguaro

(Note: 22 years later, I sprouted saved tumbleweed seeds and grew them into a 4 inch tumbleweed!)

Glendale Walk Holding Tank Observations:

· Watering in the a.m. and again in the evening was necessary.

· Pruning and removing dead debris and leaves was also a must.

· New plants were added slowly over the weeks from field trips.

· Potting does not slow down the process of growth. Plants go to maturity and develop seeds in apparently the same amount of time. I began my seed collection in the holding tank, before the walk ever began.

· Small seedlings in the holding tank area were watered even three times during the 100 plus degree days. This became a labor of real love.

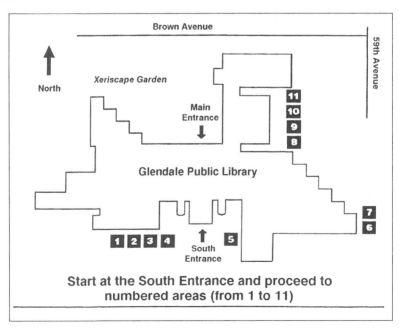

Glendale Library Walk diagram

44

Preparing the Squares

This walk included eleven 14 x 14 foot open squares in the pavement (numbers 1 through 11 in the diagram). The ground area for each was started by removing all soil and filling in the squares with potting soil and fine desert soil and lacing it with peat moss. This took quite a bit of thought and research to know how large the dirt area should be. None of us knew how much the individual plants would grow in the desert heat, even with lots of water a day.

Heavy, red, gorgeous boulders were dropped in each one of those squares, and red rock pulverized to a powder was sprinkled between the plant exhibits.

The eastern squares of the Glendale Walk.

Shown are all four of the eastern squares in which we put our exhibits. This pattern was repeated on the front side of the library, and 3 more squares between them.

45

This day heated up rapidly to 105 degrees.

This day hit 111 degrees when we spread red granite by the truckload.

A final primping by the expert David Schultz and the City of Glendale.

Dressing with powdered rock helped prevent desert "weeds" from coming up and helped keep moisture in the exhibits.

46

Research Opportunities

The city of Glendale wanted to establish the tolerance of these plants for their own reasons; I wanted to have many backups so I didn't have to go out in 110 degrees and look for similar species. How to save many plants of each of 60 or so species became the greatest research opportunity for me. Also, it became imperitive to determine how much water was needed for each exhibit area, as the underground sprinkler would have to be set accordingly for each exhibit. Additionally, some plants needed full sun, others, shade, some more water than others. The research went on and on until the big day of planting began. It took many days to complete the process and the backup plants became extremely useful over the duration of that walk and later ones.

Planting

The preparation of the beds where the exhibits were to be placed began almost immediately. Fortunately, the ground had settled quite naturally by the time we actually started planting. A step by step chart was drawn up to aid in the planting of each specie. In the larger areas planting was a week long, and by the end of it I had hundreds of plant pots left over.

For exhibits I culled out the plants that were the most healthy, and from them, a couple of additional smaller ones. More mature plants were put together and tagged for a marked exhibit, while others were cut back to grow to maturity again. I found out that if you put a plant in an exhibit with the last flowers on it, that's just an invitation for that plant to wilt and die. The solution was to include a couple of younger plants for each specie.

One thing that I want to mention to you that I learned during the early phase of this desert walk has to do with two squares that had Jacaranda trees in the middle. We left them there and planted around their root systems. Unbelievable work amassed such that I suggest that you not include a Jacaranda tree in your exhibit! At a certain time of the year, tendrils and long needles around the flowers of the Jacaranda fall from the branches in great abundance. Weeks of raking, and picking the debris ensued. Every day the work schedule had to set aside an hour for this task and just as we thought things were over, the next stage of pods began. The nutlike pods fell from the twigs and in some cases, actually destroyed other seedlings.

We all learned that we had to keep these two squares pristine or else!

The Water System

David Schultz worked with assistant Richard Bond on the water system, which was an underground sprinkler system to maintain and control this mammoth "desert" walk of wild edibles. David was the water commissioner and the project was quite impossible without his help. I can never thank him enough. The plants were hand watered between problems such as water main breaks, "bubbler" emitter breaks, underground leaks, etc. All were a weekly challenge.

Tools

We used quite a number of different kinds of tools, and here's a drawing I did to show what is minimally needed for a walk of this size. These items were in our shed that was attached to this walk.

Left to right: Scissors, favorite shovel, clippers, favorite pitchfork, pails, screens, pointed trowel, container of spoons, small hand rake, dandelion puller, small flat shovel, pile of branches or dowels used as stakes, hand saw, broom.

The Signs Project

Each plant exhibit needs its own sign, so we gave the names of the plants and other info to the sign manufacturer. Many weeks passed before the walk was actually ready, and during that time the signs were being made by the city of Glendale. The signs were cut by laser on special plastic that was completely heatproof and waterproof. They were tested outside during many days of intense heat. They never faded or peeled.

When they were finally ready, I was given the job of peeling the paper backing off, which exposed probably the strongest glue I have ever worked with. Then the sign was centered and pushed onto the steel frame. If it stuck on at any slight angle, that was a mistake and also no one could ever take it off because of that glue.

We tried once, working as fast as we could, but the sign still cracked off at the edge.

A group of agriculture students from Peoria High School helped with the gluing and placement of the signs for the exhibits. Honestly, without their help I could not have completed this project. Kudos!

Each sign was a red, yellow or green color, to convey specific messages. A red sign meant to stop and read it very carefully. Yellow meant to slow down and read carefully, and green meant that plant was safe to eat in suggested amounts. (Note: I always stated no more than 1/2 cup at one sitting for safety's sake. If you ate a quantity of any one plant that had a green sign, the body would just tend to cleanse, just like eating a quart of spinach for instance.)

Some exhibit signs for the Glendale walk.

Next is an alphabetical sample list of the signs (all 4" x 6") for plants whose name starts with the letters A - C, plus its Latin name and the sign color.

PLANT LATIN NAME	SIGN COLOR
Alfalfa, *lucerne sativa*	yellow
Aloe, coral, *aloe barbandensis*	yellow
Aloe vera, *aloe barbandensis*	yellow
Aloe, soapy, *aloe saponaria*	yellow
Amaranth, globe, *gomphrene globosa*	green
Amaranth, Hopi red, *A. cruentus*	green
Amaranth, palmer, *amaranthus palmeri*	green
Amaranth, red root, *amaranthus retroflexus*	green
Aster, purple, *machaeranthera canescens*	yellow
Barley, hare, *hordeum leporinum*	yellow
Barnyard grass, *echinochloa crus-galli*	yellow
Bermuda grass, California, *bromus carinatus*	yellow
Blue grass, soft, *bromus mollis*	yellow
Burdock, common, *arctium minus*	yellow
Canary gross, little speed, *phalaris minor*	yellow
Cattail, *thypha latifolia*	green
Chamomile, German, *matricatia officinalis*	yellow
Cheat, *bromis secalinus*	yellow
Chia, Dapk, Indian wheat, salvia, *columbarie*	yellow
Chickweed, *stellaria media*	green
Chicory, *chichorium intybus*	green
Clover, red, *trifolium pratense*	yellow
Clover, white, *trifolium alba*	yellow

That is how you could set up signs for a very large identification walk. Plants that would have a red sign would be nettles, willow and milkweed, for example.

Insect Control

This was a really big problem in a desert hot summer because of these common enemies: spider mites, fungus gnats, white flies, aphids, mealy bugs, Japanese beetles, red ants, black ants, fire ants, caterpillars.

To deal with the devastation caused by the white fly, we had to make gigantic batches of garlic, olive oil and dish soap, each 1/3 of the mixture. This concoction kept the Arizona white fly from eating the succulent new young seedlings plus we had to use it to go over every exhibit after the first hit from the flies. It took twice a day for three or four days but those flies finally gave up and the plants began to grow again. The white flies tried twice more in July, but we were ready for them and the invasion was stopped by our "salad" recipe. The flies simply slipped off the leaves!

I have since used this recipe on roses back in the eastern U.S. and it is just as effective on Japanese beetles as on white flies out west. Insecticidal soap in water makes a wonderful solution to spray on plants as well. Continual dousings by me, David Schultz and his wife Joan kept the desert walk lush and green so that the public viewed a pristine plant walk for their identification. (Note: I suggest you not leave the garlic, soap and oil mixture inside a shed where it could become an unpleasant odor to visitors.)

Red spider mites were controlled also, as the hot weather brought them out in force. I did find a few black widow nests and a couple of brown recluses which were immediately destroyed. We did not eat from this walk as the exhibits were for identification only, though we did have to harvest the exhibits when they got too overgrown.

Other common live problems to any walk can include scorpions, rabbits, dogs, deer, peacocks, turtles, rodents, etc. Some will be more prevalent in certain areas but you should plan on having to deal with them at some time or other, and your choice of edgings and boundaries can be a deterrent.

Dealing with Desert Soil

Desert soil or caliche soil is very hard to dig. Sand has pressed into a clay-like surface. I had bent spoons and trowels trying to dig this soil. One way to dig it out is to wet it down. When you do water this soil, the water runs off like it is on cement. When we wanted to plant something in its native soil for research, we actually hosed down a section of sand, letting the hose drip slowly for some time, then dug with a shovel and filled our plastic pots. Because the soil does harden so firmly, we chose not to use it in the walk in any case. It was easier and less risky to use farm topsoil, or fertile top soil. Loamy soil is much like commercial potting soil so there is no caliche soil in that.

Desert Grasses and Other Grasses

In the next photo you can see that the rims of the black pots are still visible. Those containers were covered entirely after the grasses were put in and the red dirt distributed.

Grass exhibit before dressing of red rock powder.

After the walk opened and when we had students visit this exhibit, they were encouraged to take grass samples, make notebooks, and follow the information in our hand-out materials regarding grass edibility and how to cook them. Sorrel, for instance, should be cooked briefly. For panic grass and rat-tail fesque, we cleaned

Some grasses that were ground to flour make delicious muffins, cookies, ect.

them up and placed them in trays to dry. Part of the appeal of grasses is that they are easy to cut, dry, and grind for flour. Eventually all specimens of grasses were ground for a taste test, and crabgrass and nut sedges, as well as bulrush, were always voted the best tasting.

Some grasses were planted before others that did not germinate until the cooler months. The list of grasses that were on exhibit in the Glendale Walk can be found in the brochure pages, "City of Glendale Edible Wild Plant Walk," which is reproduced later in this section.

As a caution, the red signs in the exhibit stated that the black mold that might form between the seeds of grasses is not edible and one should examine the grass closely before eating, drying, or reducing to flour for baking. The #1 rule in grass gathering is to look out for black dots, any time of the year. Any black dots? If so, discard, please.

Here also is another caution about certain grasses. *The Essential Wild Food Survival Guide* mentions velvet grass and stink grass as toxic because the physical seed heads collect mold easily and stink grass does smell bad. I did not mention the grass named Johnson grass as being a problem because at the time I didn't know there might be one. For years I harvested the tops of Johnson grass; I made gallons of flour out of it and used that to make cookies and breads. But one day I opened my mail and a letter stated that Johnson grass made cyanide when its leaves and stems got bent in some way. I looked up this fact in many research books found in the Biosphere data banks, and sure enough, I did find the information that cyanide in tiny amounts was made when the stalk was bent over, from wind, deer, ect., or from hot, dry conditions. Just the thought of possible harm from this grass made me stop using and talking about it.

The Cattail and Sunflower Exhibits

Before we opened the walk to visitors, we knew that there was no way we could keep the exhibit wet enough for cattails, so we used a dry exhibit that was very easy to install. The following steps for cattail are ones that I did for other walks as well. I used an old basket, buried it in soil and added a big bunch of cattails. Sand was poured into the buried basket with cattail stems, which secured the exhibit for a complete summer and winter. Except for excited children pulling the hotdog shaped cattail out for souvenirs, the exhibit was only refurbished once! Eventually a small stringed fence did the job.

Setting up a cattail exhibit

Sunflower plants had to be staked due to the height and weight of them. The sunflowers were wild ones, becoming 12-14 feet tall. We knew that insects had so much to gather from this exhibit, and others. We found that cautions about yellow-jackets and hornets were necessary, but no one was ever stung. Red ants

56

Cattails on exhibit. Here, the posts are ready to get their signs.

climbed bushes and reminded me of the pictures I have seen in Africa of killer ants.

Giant Sunflower   Wild Sunflower

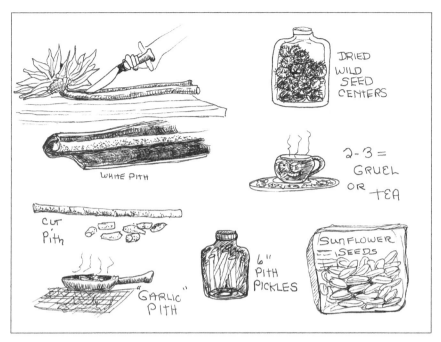

How to Use a Sunflower for Food

Arizona Master Gardeners Visit

August 10 through August 14 we prepared for a special lecture-walk of the Arizona Master Gardeners. It was fun for me to clean all exhibits, prune, when necessary, and dust off red boulders. Sidewalks were swept perfect and we even used a blower on low speed to clean debris off leaves.

On August 16 the Master Gardeners came, 82 strong. What a wonderful time we all had. I have never answered so many questions. Seeds (including blue lettuce, prickly lettuce, amaranth, Palmer amaranth, Hopi red amaranth, sow thistle, perennial lettuce) were discussed and shown in storage notebooks. I encouraged everyone to do the same any time they wanted. Pick samples, and seeds, and have your salad lunch—that is the statement we often heard.

We collected seeds from a Flagstaff Arboretum trip, which included pepper grass, blue aster, and red clover and planted them, and they grew prolifically.

A completed, flourishing square

Upper left shows broad leaf sorrel. Lower left, garden sorrel. In rear on right, field sorrel. Front, a large patch of common purslane, and another large specie, known as horse purslane specie.

59

To prepare for the expected walk-lecture (90 people) we did another complete pruning, cleaning, and restringing of bushes for it.

The first walk, where 90 people showed up! They took turns surrounding a square so others could see.

Typical lecture during an identification walk.

Visitors . . .

and more visitors .

Inspecting the grass exhibit.

Summary of General Preparation Steps for the Glendale Arizona Walk

1. Soil tilled, additives (peat moss, potting soil, etc.) worked in.

2. Sign posts drilled.

3. Heavy rocks for decoration put in exhibit areas using a front loader.

4. Automatic drip system put in place.

5. Plants taken from the holding tank and planted. (We did a dozen or so a day.)

6. Red crushed granite for long-lasting beauty added to the exhibit.

62

7. Bubbler system adjusted until we had 5 gallons of water per exhibit per day.

8. Tackled the problem of dealing with white flies (detailed on page 58), and addressed other insect problems as well.

9. Started the ongoing weeding of the weeds.

10. Began the daily inspection of the walk area and remove any garbage, trash, etc., from it.

11. For any areas that might need some fill in, we planted finished plants from the holding tank.

Our Most Successful Exhibit

The amaranth exhibit was the most successful by far. The Hopi red amaranth, the most nutritious and colorful plant in the entire exhibit, grew 10-12 feet tall. All types of amaranth were abundant, but the Hopi red became the talk of the area! Harvest became a weekly

The red amaranth exhibit.

job; the hotter it got, the more the plants grew. One can harvest such a plant hundreds of times if one wants to, and we all had enough amaranth for a year or so. Lamb's quarters was also in this exhibit but grew to normal sizes, unlike the prolific amaranth.

This well-known plant that grows on the Mesa and in Navaho country was familiar to the Aztecs as well. We found that one amaranth seed head was enough for a loaf of bread, and we were able to gather over 4 gallons of flour from the heads of the plants.

The Hopi red amanarth before the signs were put on

One of the reasons this was such a successful walk and so many people enjoyed it was because we handed out our "City of Glendale Edible Wild Plant Walk" brochure. I have reproduced it for you, in case it is useful to you as an example of something that you can put together for your walk visitors.

City of Glendale Edible Wild Plant Walk

at the Glendale Public Library
5959 West Brown Avenue
Glendale, Arizona 85302

City of Glendale
Edible Wild Plant Walk

Color coded for your added safety:
YELLOW – CAUTION read carefully
GREEN – Go, safe
RED – STOP! read specific CAUTION

Located on South and East sides of the Glendale Public Library
on Brown Avenue (1st light S. of Peoria)
5959 West Brown Avenue
Glendale, Arizona

The **NATIVE, NATURAL WILD FOOD WALK** is comprised of eleven 13' x 13' squares planted
with 102 species of edible plants. Each plant sign is color coded. **PLEASE DO NOT EAT
OUR SAMPLES!**

"Puffy Pete" shows the **YELLOW**-caution sign, slow down and read carefully. **GREEN**-go, most
indications show small amounts are safe to eat. **RED**-stop, read carefully for the **CAUTION**
specific to these plants.

The signs are important for your individual safety. Most important, READ THE FORAGING RULES
(Page 2). State rules apply to our deserts. One may not remove cactus or trees, bushes
without State permits. Buds and extensions used for food in survival situations are allowed.
City rules have an 18-inch height for "weeds". They must be cut after this, for your own
safety, fire safety, etc. To use native foods for your family is as simple as farming the
plants. Our squares are examples of this. Perhaps using rocks around your food plant is
all that would be necessary for harvesting a large wild lettuce, for instance.

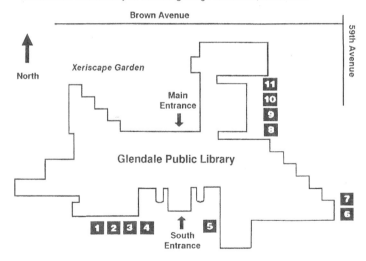

Start at the South Entrance and proceed to
numbered areas (from 1 to 11)

cover only 2606 12/95   1

RULES OF FORAGING

I. **DO NOT** collect plants closer than 100 feet from a car path or contaminated area.

2. **NEVER** collect from areas sprayed with herbicides, pesticides, or other chemicals.

3. **DO NOT** collect plants with **RED STEMS,** or red striations or stripes. All weeds tend to pull up nitrates from the desert soil which turns the stems red.

4. **ALWAYS** be familiar with all dangerous plants in **YOUR** area of collection.

5. **POSITIVELY IDENTIFY ALL PLANTS** you intend to use for **FOOD**.

6. **TAKE A PIECE OFF THE PLANT AND ROLL BETWEEN YOUR FINGERS.** Sniff carefully. Does it smell like something you would eat? If it doesn't, **DISCARD IMMEDIATELY.** If it does, **GO ON TO THE NEXT RULE.**

7. **TAKE ANOTHER PIECE OFF THE PLANT AND ROLL UNTIL JUICY. RUB THE** tiny piece on your gums above your teeth.

8. **WAIT** 20 minutes.

9. **DOES YOUR GUM ITCH, BURN, TINGLE, SWELL OR STING?** If no outward reaction occurs, **GO ON TO THE NEXT RULE**.

10. **TAKE ANOTHER PIECE OF THE PLANT AND PUT IN A TEACUP. ADD BOILING WATER AND STEEP FOR 5 MINUTES. SIP SLOWLY FOR 20** more minutes. **WATCH for NAUSEA, BURNING, DISCOM-FORT. IF NO OUTWARD REACTION OCCURS, YOU MAY INGEST A SMALL AMOUNT.**

11. **WAIT ANOTHER 20 MINUTES AND WATCH FOR ANY OUTWARD REACTION.**

12. **KEEP ALL SAMPLES AWAY FROM CHILDREN OR PETS.**

13. **STORE ALL SEEDS AND BULBS AWAY FROM CHILDREN AND PETS.**

14. **TEACH CHILDREN TO KEEP** all plants away from their mouths and **DO NOT LET** children chew or suck nectar from any unknown plants.

15. **AVOID SMOKE FROM BURNING PLANTS. SMOKE MAY IRRITATE THE EYES OR CAUSE ALLERGIC REACTIONS QUICKLY.**

16. **BE AWARE OF YOUR NEIGHBOR'S HABITS** with chemicals, pesticides and herbicides.

17. **BEWARE; HEATING OR BOILING DOESN'T ALWAYS DESTROY TOXICITY.**

18. **CALL AND REPORT CHEMICAL SPILLS, ILLEGAL DUMPING, CON-TAMINATED AREAS AND ANYTHING ELSE THAT MIGHT AFFECT SAFETY TO CHILDREN AND ADULTS, AS WELL AS PLANTS.**

19. **KEEP EDIBLES SEPARATE** from **SAMPLES TO BE IDENTIFIED AND USE SEPARATE BAGS WHENEVER POSSIBLE. POISONS WILL GIVE THEIR BAD QUALITIES TO FOOD IN THE SAME BAG PROXIMITY.**

2

67

Edible Wild Plant Walk
Numerical list of edible plants

1. PURPLE NUTSEDGE, *Cyperus rotundus*
2. HARE BARLEY, *Hordeum leporinum*
3. QUACKGRASS, *Elytrigia repens*
4. SOFT BROMEGRASS, *Bromus mollis*
5. ANNUAL BLUEGRASS, *Poa annua*
6 . ITALIAN RYEGRASS, *Lolium multiflorum*
7. GREEN FOXTAIL, *Setaria viridis*

8. SOAPY ALOE, *Aloe saponaria*
9. CORAL ALOE, *Aloe mitriformis*

10. **ALOE VERA-MEDICINAL,** *Aloe barbandensis*
CAUTION: GEL IS BITTER AND ONLY YOUNG LEAVES ARE USED FOR MEDICINAL PUR-
POSES, AS WELL AS SURVIVAL FOOD.
EDIBLE PARTS: Flowers and very young leaves
USES: <u>Flowers:</u> Raw; salads; teas. Freeze in ice cubes or as popsicles. Freeze for long term
storage. <u>Young leaves:</u> Lay flat side down, skin off the tough outer layer. Expose the gel.
Scrape the gel out with a spoon and add to orange juice. Freeze gel in ice cube tray for
long term storage.

(8., 9., 10.) Aloe Vera Morning Tonic

1 aloe vera ice cube
3/4 cup fresh orange juice
Combine ice cube and orange juice in a glass. Let cube melt, then drink. Serves 1.
HINT: To make cubes, place an aloe vera leaf on its flat side and peel the skin off with a
sharp knife. Scrape the gel with a spoon, holding on to one end of the leaf. Place the gel into
ice cube trays and freeze.

---

11. **EPHEDRA-MORMON TEA,** *Ephedra torreyana*
CAUTION: DRINK SMALL AMOUNTS OF TEA AT FIRST.
EDIBLE PARTS: Twigs, stems, branch parts, and seeds
USES: <u>Twigs, branches, stems:</u> Beverage; teas. (Weak teas at first)
<u>Seeds:</u> Grind as flour additive. Dry for long term storage.

---
11. Ephedra Tea

Break a handful of twigs into a pot. Cover with water and bring to a boil. Turn off heat,
cover and steep 10 minutes.

---

12. **BLUE ASTER,** *Machaeranthera canescens*
EDIBLE PARTS: Leaves, young flowers
USES: <u>Young leaves:</u> Vegetable; raw; salads; sandwiches. Cook in soups; crockpot; main dishes.
Dry or freeze for long term storage. <u>Flowers:</u> Raw; salads. Dry or freeze for long term
storage.

---
12. Blue Aster Vegetable

Leaves and flowers, any color Wild Aster.
Chop fine. Steam for 10 minutes, and serve as vegetable. Dry and add as a pinch of
seasoning.

---

13. **CHIA-DAPK-INDIAN WHEAT**, *Salvia columbarie*
EDIBLE PARTS: Seeds
USES: <u>Seeds:</u> Raw; salads; jello; beverage. Dry for long term storage.

-3-

13. Chia Seasoning

Sprinkle seeds on anything! Nutritious.

14. VIOLETS, *Viola semperflorens*
EDIBLE PARTS: All
USES: Flowers: Raw; salads; teas. Freeze in ice cubes or as popsicles. Decorate cakes, candy. Freeze for long term storage. Leaves: Vegetable; raw; salads; sandwiches. Cook in soups and stews. Dry for flour additive. Freeze for long term storage.

14. Violet Ice Cream

A handful of blossoms in vanilla ice cream can be of great interest to a child! Leaves may be cooked and eaten like spinach.

15. MEXICAN EVENING PRIMROSE, *Oenothera berlandieri*
EDIBLE PARTS: Flowers, seeds, roots
USES: Flowers: Raw; salads; teas; jellies and oils. Freeze in ice cubes or as popsicles. Seeds: Grind for a food additive. Salad dressings. Spread on baked goods. Roots: Old roots need to be parboiled to remove sharp taste. Young roots: raw in salads. Cook in soups and stews. Freeze for long term storage.

15. Evening Primrose Olive Oil

Fill a 10-ounce jar to capacity with washed flowers. Add extra virgin olive oil to cover. Repeatedly press flowers until all air bubbles are out of mixture. Cap and shake every day for 2 weeks. Remove flowers and discard. Use for salads. (makes approx. 10 ounces.)

16. WHITE CLOVER, *Trifolium alba (Right)*

17. RED CLOVER Trifolium pratense (Left)
EDIBLE PARTS: All (Small amounts only)
USES: Flowers: Raw; salads; teas. Freeze in ice cubes or as popsicles. Decorate cakes, candy. Dry or freeze for long term storage. Leaves: Vegetable; raw; salads; sandwiches. Cook in soups and stews. Dry or freeze for long term storage.

16. & 17. Frozen Clover

Clover can be frozen by placing it in a single layer on freezer wrap, folding over two sides to hold the clover in place. Roll the paper to make a compact package, fasten and freeze.

18. SHEPHERD'S PURSE, *Capsella bursa pastoris*
EDIBLE PARTS: All
USES: Seeds: Add to soups, eggs, potato salad, etc. Leaves: Vegetable; raw; salads; sandwiches. Cook in soups and stews. Dry or freeze for long term storage.

18. Shepherd's purse Sandwich

Pick young leaves and wash thoroughly. Place leaves in a sandwich and use as lettuce. Enjoy!

19. REDSTEM FILAREE, *Erodium cicutarium*
CAUTION: DO NOT EAT FLOWERS OR STORKBILL SEEDS. MAY BE TOXIC. ALSO, DO NOT EAT RED STEMS OF RED LEAVES. ONLY EAT GREEN, YOUNG LEAVES.
EDIBLE PARTS: Leaves and roots
USES: Leaves: Vegetable; raw; salads; sandwiches. Cook in soups and stews. (Use as a celery flavored substitute). Dry or freeze for long term storage. Roots: Vegetable; raw. Cook in soups and stews; crockpot. Freeze for long term storage.

-4-

69

---

19. Filarie Sandwich

1 handful filarie leaves, washed
Pinch dried thyme leaves
1/4 teaspoon each of oil and vinegar
1 Bermuda onion, thinly sliced into rings
2 slices whole wheat bread
    Layer ingredients between the bread slices for a "desert sandwich" treat. Makes 1 sandwich.

---

20. CATTAIL, *Thypha latifolia*
EDIBLE PARTS: All at all stages
USES: <u>Early shoots:</u> Vegetable; raw; salads. <u>Early pollen:</u> Raw. Cook into pancakes, muffins.
    Small amounts at first. <u>Green pod:</u> As corn on the cob. <u>Pith:</u> Center of a mature stem,
    peel and eat; vegetable; raw; salads; pickles. <u>Early brown cob:</u> Immediately after cob turns
    brown, harvest, dry, and grind to flour. Freeze for long term storage. <u>Roots:</u> Raw. Pound
    to fiber. Dry, grind into flour. <u>Fluff:</u> After cob turns to seed, use fluff for stuffing, life jackets
    and floatation clothing.

---

20. Cattail "Corn On The Cob"!

2 or 3 green cattail heads
Safflower or olive oil, or butter
Salt or Queen Anne's lace seeds
Thyme pepper (optional)
    Put the cattail in a large pot of boiling water and boil for 7 minutes. Remove and serve with
oil or butter, salt or seeds, and thyme. Serves one as a side dish.

NOTE: When cutting, leave 2 inches of stem for holding the cob.

---

21. MALLOW, *Malva neglecta*
EDIBLE PARTS: All
USES: <u>Seeds:</u> Raw; salads; eggs; etc. Cook in soups and stews; stir-fry. Grind into flour. Dry or
    freeze for long term storage. <u>Leaves:</u> Vegetable; raw; salads; sandwiches. Cook in soups
    and stews; stir-fry. Dry, grind into flour. Freeze for long term storage. <u>Stems:</u> Vegetable;
    raw. Cut into bean size sections for stir-fry. Dry for long term storage. <u>Roots:</u> Raw; salads;
    french-fry. Dry or freeze for long term storage.

---

21. Stuffed Mallow

Wash and stem 10 or 12 Mallow leaves
Place 1 tablespoon refried beans in center and roll
Put in baking dish with folded side down. Cover with salsa.
Bake at 350 degrees for 30 minutes or until bubbly.

NOTE: This dish may be frozen and then baked later.

---

22. SPEARMINT *Mint spicata* (Right)

23. MINT *Mint arvensis* (Left)
EDIBLE PARTS: All
NOTE: All mints have a SQUARE STEM. There are dozens of varieties.
USES: <u>Leaves:</u> Raw; salads; teas. Freeze in ice cubes or as popsicles. Chew a couple of leaves
    for gum. Dry or freeze for long term storage. <u>Flowers:</u> Raw; salads; teas. Freeze in ice
    cubes or as popsicles. Decorate cakes, candy. Dry or freeze for long term storage.

22., 23., 26. Mint Popsicles

1 handful mint leaves, washed Mint leaves for garnish
    Place mint in a pot and add boiling water to cover. Cover the pot tightly and steep for 10
to 15 minutes. Strain, cool, pour the liquid into popsicle molds. Place a leaf in each mold
and freeze. (Makes 6 popsicles.) If you don't have popsicle molds, freeze in ice cube trays,
adding a mint leaf to each cube. This is delicious in iced tea and other beverages.

-5-

70

24. ALFALFA, *Lucerne medicago sativa*
EDIBLE PARTS: Young leaves and flowers (Small amounts only)
USES: Flowers: Raw; salads; teas. Freeze in ice cubes or as popsicles. Dry or freeze
    for long term storage. Leaves: Vegetable; raw; salads; sandwiches. Cook
    in soups and stews. Dry or freeze for long term storage.

24. Alfalfa Tea

Take 1/4 cup flowers and small leaves, wash. Place in pot and cover with boiling water.
Steep 5 minutes. Makes 1 cup of tea. Drink hot or cold.

25. TUMBLEWEED-RUSSIAN THISTLE, *Salsola iberica*
CAUTION: DO NOT EAT PLANTS WITH RED OR PURPLE STRIPES ON STEMS. THIS MEANS
    THE PLANT HAS PULLED UP HARMFUL NITRATES FROM THE SOIL.
EDIBLE PARTS: All
USES: Leaves: Vegetable; teas. Cook in soup and stews; crockpot. Clip and cook the last 2 inches
    of the branches (most succulent). Freeze for long term storage.

25. Tumbleweed Soup

1 cup tumbleweed tips
1 clove garlic
Water to cover
1 thinly sliced onion
    Place cup of tumbleweed tips in water to cover. Simmer for 20 minutes on low. (Crock pots
are fantastic for 1 hour on low). Add pressed oil from 1 clove of garlic. Add thinly sliced onion
and serve.

26. PEPPERMINT, *Piperita mentha*
EDIBLE PARTS: All
NOTE: All mints have a SQUARE STEM.
USES: Leaves: Raw; salads; teas. Freeze in ice cubes or as popsicles. Chew a couple of leaves
    for gum. Dry or freeze for long term storage. Flowers: Raw; salads, teas. Freeze in ice
    cubes or as popsicles. Decorate cakes, candy. Dry or freeze for long term storage.

26. Peppermint Garnish

Use fresh leaves as garnish. Steep in hot water to make tea. Dried leaves may be added
to potpourri.

27. ENGLISH THYME, *T. Vulgaris common* (Right)

28. MOTHER OF THYME, *T. praecox arcticus* (Left)
EDIBLE PARTS: All
USES: Whole Plant: Spice for meats, stews, main dishes, fish. Dry or freeze for long term storage.

27., 28. Thyme Pepper

Collect Thyme from your lawn, using scissors. Spread leaves and flowers on a screen to
dry. Put through a grinder when crackly dry. Use as pepper for all dishes.

29. DAY LILY, *Hemerocallis fulva*
All colors
CAUTION: SMALL AMOUNTS, EXPECIALLY ROOTS. LARGE QUANTITIES MAY CAUSE
    DIARRHEA.
EDIBLE PARTS: Flowers, buds, corm roots of some varieties
USES: Flowers: Raw; salads. Freeze in ice for long term storage. Buds: Vegetable; raw. Cooked
    in fritters and pancakes. Prepare as asparagus. Dry, store buds in glass for long term
    storage. Roots: Raw in small quantities; salads; stir-fry. Dry or freeze for long term storage.

-6-

71

---

29. Day Lily Hints

WARNING: identify carefully in photo references
Fresh buds, fry in sweet oil or put in pancake batter for a delicious pancake.
Drop buds or flowers in water for a 4-minute garnish.
Pour heated sour cream over buds or flowers, and serve.

---

30. SUNFLOWER, *Helianthus annuus*
CAUTION: Leaves, stems, and roots are NOT EDIBLE as they may pull nitrates from the soil.
EDIBLE PARTS: Seed center (Small amounts only) pith.
USES: Seed centers: Steep and drink broth. Mash and add to peanut butter, etc. Dry, store seed
heads in glass for long term storage.

30. Sunflower Soup

Collect after the flower matures and petals fall off. Wait until the petals are
wilted, take the brown dried center. Dry center further on screen before bottling.
Make soup. Pith may be collected by peeling the outer fresh stem and pulling
out the white "styrofoam-like pith." Add to soup.

---

31. OXEYE DAISY *Chrysanthemum leucanthemus* (Right)
32. ENGLISH DAISY Bellis perennis (Left)
CAUTION: DO NOT EAT DAISY CENTERS IN ANY QUANTITY
EDIBLE PARTS: Petals, leaves, stems

USES: Petals: Raw; salads; cake decorations. Freeze in ice cubes or as popsicles. Leaves:
Vegetable; raw; salads; sandwiches. Cook in soups and stews. Dry for long term storage.
Stems: Eat raw for a trail nibble.

31., 32. Daisy Jello

Why not make a treat of flower petals in salad or clear jello with petals, or
even chocolate ice cream with daisy petals.

---

33. GERMAN CHAMOMILE (CAMOMILE) *Matricaria officinalis* (Right)

34. ROMAN CHAMOMILE (CAMOMILE) *Anthemis nobilis* (Left)
EDIBLE PARTS: All (small amounts only)
USES: Flowers: Raw; salads; teas, Freeze in ice cubes or as popsicles. Dry or freeze for long
term storage. Leaves: Vegetable; raw; salads; sandwiches. Cook in soups and stews. Dry
for long term storage. Stems: Eat raw for a trail nibble. Dry for long term storage.

33., 34. Chamomile

Chamomile Tea
1/4 cup chamomile leaves and flowers, washed
2 cups water
Honey (optional)
Place chamomile in a small saucepan. Add water, bring to a boil, turn off heat, and cover.
Steep 10 min. Strain and serve with honey. Serves 1 or 2

HINT: To use as a hair rinse, simmer the entire plant in water. Cool, strain, and apply. Let
this set on your hair for a while and rinse again.

---

35. GOLDEN YARROW), *Millefolium V. aureum* (Rear

36. COMMON YARROW *Achillea millefolium* (Center)

37. RED YARROW *Millefolium V. roseum* (Lower Left)
CAUTION: ALL PARTS HAVE A STIMULANT AND DIURETIC PROPERTY. EAT IN
SMALL AMOUNTS ONLY.
EDIBLE PARTS: All (sparingly)
USES: Flowers: Tea. Dry for long term storage.
Leaves: Raw; salads; teas. 1 or 2 leaves per serving. Dry or freeze in ice for long term storage.

35., 36., 37. Yarrow Tooth Powder or Paste

1 piece of burnt toast
Yarrow leaves, dried and ground
  Scrape the charcoal off a piece of burnt toast. Make a mixture of half charcoal and half ground yarrow for a refreshing, cleansing tooth powder. Or add a small amount of water to form a paste.

  Variation: Dry a thick, straight-stemmed yarrow plant. Remove and save the leaves for tea. Cut the desired stem to the size of a toothbrush.. Using a knife, make multiple cuts on one end of stem to make a fuzzy tip. In an emergency, cut a large raw yarrow leaf and scrub your teeth by pressing the leaf on them and rubbing. Rinse.

---

38. **JUNGLERICE-WATERGRASS**, *Echinochloa colona*
39. **WITCHGRASS-TUMBLE PANIC**, *Panicum capillare*
40. **BRISTLY FOXTAIL**, *Setaria vertidillata*
41. **LARGE HAIRY CRABGRASS**, *Digitaria sanguinalis*
42. **SMOOTH CRABGRASS**, *Digitaria ischaemum*
43. **RATTAIL FESCUE**, *Vulpia myuros*
44. **CALIFORNIA BROMEGRASS**, *Bromus carinatus*
45. **UMBRELLAGRASS**, *Cyprus altermifolius*
46. **PANICGRASS**, *Sangui-Guarjio, Panicum sonorum*
47. **YELLOW FOXTAIL**, *Setaria glauca*
48. **WILD OAT**, *Arvena fatua*
49. **GOOSEGRASS**, *Eleusine indica*
50. **FALL PANICUM**, *Panicum dichotomiflorum*
51. **BARNYARDGRASS**, *Echinochloa crus--galli*
52. **MEDITERRANEANGRASS**, *Schismus barbatus*
53. **ARIZONA PANICUM**, *Panicum arizonicum*
54. **SIDEOATS GRAMA**, *Bouteloua curtipendula*
55. **BROWNTOP PANICUM**, *Panicum fasciculatum*
56. **BERMUDAGRASS**, *Cynodon dactylon*
57. **LEMONGRASS**, *Andropogon schoenanthus*
58. **LITTLESEED CANARY**, *Phalaris minor*
59. **CEREAL RYE**, *Secale cereale*
60. **SOUTHWESTERN CUPGRASS**, *Eriochloa gracilis*
61. **SPIDERGRASS**, *Aristida ternites*
62. **YELLOW NUTSEDGE**, *Cyperus esculentus*
63. **CHEAT**, *Bromus secalinus*
64. **ORCHARDGRASS**, *Daclylis glomerata*

Crabgrass Muffins

1 cup Enriched Flour
1 cup Crabgrass Flour
3/4 cup water
2 eggs
1 tsp. pure vanilla
2 tsp ginger (optional)
1/4 cup sunflower or canola oil
1/2 cup raisins
2 tsp. baking soda
  Place flours in bowl, mix in thoroughly water and add eggs (author uses egg replacer), vanilla, oil, raisins and baking soda. Fold in thoroughly. Place 1/2 full in muffin tins or pour in 8" square baking pan. Preheat oven 350°. Place in oven 20-25 minutes. Let cool and remove from tins. Makes 6 muffins.

65. **PALMER AMARANTH** (Long slender seed section), *Amaranthus palmeri*
EDIBLE PARTS: All
USES: Seed heads: Cereal; granola; flour. Raw; cooked. Grind to a flour additive.
    Salad dressings. Spread on baked goods. Dry or freeze for long term
    storage. Leaves: Vegetable; raw; salads; sandwiches. Cook in soups and
    stews. Dry or freeze for long term storage. Roots: Parboil to soften. Raw;
    salads. Cook in soups and stews. Freeze for long term storage.

66. **REDROOT AMARANTH** (Short, stubby seed section), *Amaranthus retroflexus*
EDIBLE PARTS: All
USES: Seed heads: Cereal; granola; flour. Raw; cooked. Grind to a flour additive.
    Salad dressings. Spread on baked goods. Dry or freeze for long term
    storage. Leaves: Vegetable; raw; salads; sandwiches. Cook in soups and
    stews. Dry or freeze for long term storage. Roots: Parboil to soften. Raw;
    salads. Cook in soups and stews. Freeze for long term storage.

67. **TUMBLE PIGWEED**, *Amaranthus albas*
CAUTION: DO NOT EAT RED STEMS OR LEAVES
EDIBLE PARTS: All
USES: Seed Heads: Cereal; granola; flour. Raw; cooked. Grind to a flour
    additive. Salad dressings. Spread on baked goods. Dry or freeze for
    long germ storage. Leaves: Vegetable; raw; salads; sandwiches. Cook
    in soups and stews. Dry or freeze for long term storage. Roots: Parboil
    to soften. Raw; salads. Cook in soups and stews. Freeze for long term storage.

65., 66., 67., 70., 71. Amaranth Wild Muffins

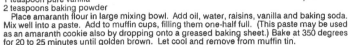

1-3/4 cups amaranth flower
1/4 cup olive oil or sunflower oil
3/4 cup water
1/2 cup raisins (optional)
1 teaspoon pure vanilla
2 teaspoons baking powder
  Place amaranth flour in large mixing bowl. Add oil, water, raisins, vanilla and baking soda. Mix well into a paste. Add to muffin cups, filling them one-half full. (This paste may be used as an amaranth cookie also by dropping onto a greased baking sheet.) Bake at 350 degrees for 20 to 25 minutes until golden brown. Let cool and remove from muffin tin.
  For those allergic to grain, please note amaranth is a vegetable plant, not a grain. Beginners can start with 25 to 75 percent non-grain soya flour or potato flour.

68. LAMBSQUARTERS-GOOSEFOOT *Chenopodium alba* (Left)
CAUTION: AVOID EATING PLANTS WITH RED STEMS OR LEAVES. (As a flour, use sparingly
        and gradually build up amount)
EDIBLE PARTS: All
USES: Seeds: Grind to a paste. Cereal; granola; hot mush. Dry and grind to flour. Dry or freeze for long term storage. Leaves: Vegetable; raw; salads. Cook in soups and stews; stir-fry. Dry or freeze for long term storage. Roots: Cook to softer consistancy in stews and crockpot. Dry or freeze for long term storage.

68., 69. Lambs Quarters Left-Overs

  HINT: Pinch the tops and tips of each branch. Wait two or three days, then repeat. For each tip you take, two or three will grow in its place. Just a few plants will yield an entire ongoing spring and summer supply.
  Lamb's Quarters leftovers. Chop vegetable, and serve cold with oil and vinegar as a garnish. Add chopped onion if you wish. Serves as delicious, nutritious side dish.
  Lamb's Quarters tops. Fill your favorite pot with tops, leaves, and seeds. Cover with water. Simmer 7 minutes. Drain, and add your favorite seasoning. Serve hot.

69. NARROWLEAF GOOSEFOOT *Chenopodium desiccatum* (Right)
CAUTION: AVOID EATING PLANTS WITH RED STEMS OR LEAVES.
(As a flour, use sparingly and gradually build up amount)
EDIBLE PARTS: All
USES: Seeds: Grind to a paste. Cereal; granola; hot mush. Dry and grind to flour. Dry or freeze for long term storage. Leaves: Vegetable; raw; salads. Cook in soups and stews; stir-fry. Dry or freeze for long term storage. Roots: Cook to softer consistancy in stews and crockpot. Dry or freeze for long term storage.

70. HOPI RED AMARANTH *A. cruentus* (Left)

71. GRAIN AMARANTH (Golden) A. hypochondriacus (Right)
EDIBLE PARTS: All
USES: Seed Heads: Dry for cereal, granola, flour. Raw; cooked. Dry or freeze for long term storage. Roots: Vegetable. Cook in soups and stews; crockpot. Freeze for long term storage. Leaves: Vegetable; raw; salads; sandwiches. Cook in soups and stews. Dry or freeze for long term storage.
(See above for Amaranth recipe)

72. HORSE PURSLANE (Large paddle-shaped leaves), *Trianthema portulacastrum*

73. COMMON PURSLANE (Small paddle-shaped leaves), *Portulaca oleracea*
CAUTION: DO NOT EAT PLANT IF THE STEMS HAVE TURNED RED. HORSE PURSLANE
    MAY HAVE A SALTY TASTE. AVOID QUANTITIES IF TASTE IS SALTY.
EDIBLE PARTS: All
USES: Whole plant: Vegetable; raw; salads. Cook in soups and stews; stir-fry. Pickles, known as pussley. Freeze for long term storage.

72., 73. Purslane Vertalogas

4 cups of washed purslane
1 egg, beaten (optional)
1/2 cup finely mashed breadcrumbs
1 teaspoon of peanut or olive oil
   Chop purslane finely, stems and all. Add egg, bread crumbs and your favorite seasongs.
Bake in well greased dish at 300 degrees for 20 minutes until piping hot.   Serves 4.

74. BROADLEAF SORREL, *Rumex obtusifolius* (Upper Right)

75. SHEEP SORREL, *Rumex acetosella* (Left)

76. GARDEN SORREL, *Rumex acetosa* (Lower Right)
**CAUTION: ALWAYS COOK SORREL. DO NOT EAT RAW. CONTAINS OXALIC ACID CRYS-
   TALS AND MAY BE HARMFUL TO THE KIDNEYS WHEN EATEN RAW IN LARGE
   QUANTITIES.**
EDIBLE PARTS: All
USES: <u>Flowers:</u> As a spice. Cook in soups; salads. Use less than 1 teaspoon raw. <u>Leaves:</u>
   Vegetable. Cook in soups and stews; stir-fry. Drop in boiling water for a minute or two.
   Leaf will change color. Boiling destroys the oxalic acid crystals immediately. Dry or freeze
   for long term storage. <u>Seeds:</u> As a spice. Salads. Cook in soups. Use less than 1/4
   teaspoon raw. Dry for long term storage.

74., 75. French Sorrel Soup

1 cup fresh sorrel leaves, flowers, stems
Water to cover
1 thinly sliced onion
   Place sorrel leaves in a pot and cover with water. Add onion and simmer for a few
minutes. LEAVES WILL TURN AN OLIVE GREEN from a bright green. THIS IS
NORMAL and insures you the oxalic acid crystals are destroyed. Serve hot!

77. BROADLEAF PLANTAIN (Turnip-like leaves), *Plantago major*

78. BUCKHORN PLANTAIN (Blue/grey leaves), *Plantago lancelota*

79. WOOLEY PLANTAIN (Fuzzy leaves), *Plantago patagonica*
CAUTION: MAY HAVE A LAXITIVE EFFECT OVER A TEASPOON IN QUANTITY.
EDIBLE PARTS: All
USES: <u>Seeds:</u> Spice in soups. Raw; dried. Psyllium is the same as these seeds. Dry for long
   term storage. <u>Leaves:</u> Vegetable; raw; salads; sandwiches. Cook in soups and stews. Dry
   or freeze for long term storage.

77., 78., 79. Plantain Raisin Cookies

2 cups whole wheat flour
3/4 cup dried or fresh plantain seeds
4 tablespoons baking powder
2 tablespoons molasses
1/2 cup carob-covered raisins
   Preheat the oven to 350 degrees. Mix all the ingredients in a big bowl. Add
water slowly to form a thick, pasty batter. Roll a pinch of dough between your
palms and press onto a greased baking sheet. Continue to form cookies, then
bake for 15 minutes or until golden brown. Makes 2 dozen small cookies.

80. QUEEN ANNE'S LACE, WILD CARROT, *Daucus carota*
**CAUTION: ALWAYS CRUSH AND SNIFF PLANT PART FOR A CHARACTERISTIC CARROT
   SMELL AND CHECK STEMS FOR CHARACTERISTIC TINY HAIRS. THE TINY HAIRS
   DISTINGUISH THIS FOOD FROM A DANGERIOUSLY POISONOUS SMOOTH STEM
   LOOK-ALIKE CALLED "POISON HEMLOCK".**
EDIBLE PARTS: Roots, leaves and flowers
USES: <u>Seeds:</u> Tiny amounts of dried seeds may be used as a salt substitute. <u>Leaves:</u> Vegetable;
   raw; salads. Cook in soups and stews; stir-fry. Dry or freeze for long term storage. <u>Roots:</u>
   As you would a carrot. Vegetable; raw;
shredded. Cook in soups and stews; stir-fry. Freeze for long term storage.

75

80. Wild Carrot (Queen Anne's Lace) Salt

Collect in early fall when the seed heads look like a "birdcage" and the seeds turn a light brown color. Pull upon the curled nest "popping" the head into your hand, and pulling the seeds off easily. Carry a jar with you. When you spread out your collection of seeds remove the tiny stems and twigs. Place seeds on a tray and put in oven at 250 degrees for 5 minutes, or put on a tray and place it in a warm area until completely dry. Store in glass. This salt substitute lasts for years.

81. COMMON BURDOCK, *Arctium minus*
CAUTION: EAT RAW IN SMALL AMOUNTS AS A SURVIVAL FOOD ONLY.
EDIBLE PARTS: Young leaves, flowers, peeled stalks, roots and burr centers
USES: <u>Whole plant:</u> Vegetable. Boil in several changes of water. <u>Root and pith:</u> Peel center of stem and root. Slice thin, add to stir-fry. Called El Gobo in oriental dishes. Stalks are boiled and made into BURDOCK CANDY. Dry or freeze for long term storage.

82. YELLOW SWEET CLOVER, *Melilotus officinalis*
CAUTION: EMERGENCY FOOD ONLY. MAY CONTAIN COUMARIN WHICH CAN INTERFERE WITH BLOOD CLOTTING.
EDIBLE PARTS: Flowers and leaves (Small amounts only)

82. Yellow Sweet Clover

Not a food.
Collect two cups yellow flowers. Cover with water, simmer on lowest setting. Skim any surface oil with a teaspoon. Use oil as vanilla substitute in small quantities.

USES: <u>Flowers:</u> Teas; salads; vanilla substitute. <u>Leaves:</u> Vegetable; raw; salads; sandwiches. Cook in soups and stews. Dry or freeze for long term storage.

83. DANDELION, *Taraxacum officinale*
EDIBLE PARTS: All
USES: <u>Flowers:</u> Raw; salads; teas; jellies and jams. Freeze in ice cubes or as popsicles. <u>Stems:</u> Chew raw sections as gum. Cut into bean size for stir-fry. <u>Leaves:</u> Vegetable; raw; salads; teas; stir-fry. Cook in soups and stews. Dry or freeze for long term storage. <u>Roots:</u> Vegetable; raw; salads; french-fry. Dry or freeze for long term storage.

83. Dandelion Casserole

2 cups dandelion leaves, washed
1 cup whole wheat bread crumbs
2 cups water
Preheat oven to 350 degrees and grease a 1-quart casserole dish. Put the leaves in a 1-quart saucepan and add water to cover. Simmer gently for 20 minutes, then drain, reserving the liquid. Chop the leaves fine and pour into the casserole dish. Add the reserved liquid and top with the ' bread crumbs. Bake for 25 minutes or until brown on top. Serves 3-4 as a main course.

84. BLUE LETTUCE, *Lactuca pulchella* (Right),

85. PRICKLY LETTUCE, *Lactuca serriola* (Left)
EDIBLE PARTS: All
USES: <u>Flowers:</u> Raw; salads; stir-fry; teas; jellies. Freeze in ice cubes or place in oils. <u>Leaves:</u> With Prickly Lettuce, boil until prickles dissolve, or cut off prickles with scizzors. Vegetable; raw; salads; sandwiches. Cook in soups and stews. Dry or freeze for long term storage. <u>Roots:</u> Old roots need to be parboiled to soften. Young roots: Raw in salads. Cook in soups and stews. Freeze for long term storage.

86. BLESSED THISTLE, *Cnicus benedictus* (Front right)
EDIBLE PARTS: All
USES: <u>Flower bulb:</u> Vegetable; raw or steam and break open, removing white pulp. Salads; stir-fry; teas. <u>Leaves:</u> Vegetable; raw. Cook in soups and stews; teas. Cooking will dissolve prickles. For ease, dry and grind to a powder. Flour additive. Dry or freeze for long term storage. <u>Roots:</u> Raw. Cook in soups and stews; crockpot. Freeze for long term storage.

84., 85. Wild Lettuce Salad

1 cup wild lettuce leaves, washed
1/2 cup wild lettuce buds and flowers, washed
1/2 cup shredded red cabbage
1 garlic clove, crushed
1 teaspoon wild thyme leaves fresh or dried
3 tablespoons oil
3 tablespoons vinegar of choice
  Combine all ingredients in a salad bowl, toss gently, and serve. Serves 4.

87. SPINY SOWTHISTLE, Sonchus asper
CAUTION: WATCH OUT FOR PRICKLES ON TIPS OF LEAVES. CUT OFF OR COOK TO DISSOLVE.
EDIBLE PARTS: All
USES: <u>Flowers:</u> Pull fluff from center and eat raw. <u>Leaves:</u> Vegetable; raw. Cook in soups and stews; crockpot. Dry or freeze for long term storage. <u>Roots:</u> Vegetable; raw. Cook in soups and stews; crockpot. Freeze for long term storage.

---

87. Spiny   Sowthistle Stir-Fry

1/2 cup Spring Sowthistle buds and flowers
1/2 cup red cabbage
1 clove garlic, pressed
1 teaspoon wild thyme
3 tablespoons oil and vinegar
  Add all ingredients in a salad bowl, toss gently and serve.

---

88. SAND PEPPERGRASS, *Lepidium lasiocarpum*
EDIBLE PARTS: All (Small Amounts only)
USES: <u>Seeds:</u> Pepper, sprinkle on eggs, pizza, meats, potato salad, etc. Raw; dried. Dry, store in glass shaker. <u>Leaves:</u> Vegetable; raw; salads; sandwiches. Cook in soups and stews. Dry or freeze for long term storage.

---

88. Peppergrass Spice

See 27. & 28. same uses.

---

89. CHICKWEED, *Stellaria media*
EDIBLE PARTS: All
USES: <u>Whole Plant:</u> Vegetable; raw; salads; sandwiches. Cook in soups; crockpot; main dishes. Dry or freeze for long term storage.

---

89. Chickweed Salad

1 garlic clove, peeled
1 quart loosely packed chickweed plant (no roots), washed and chopped
2 hard-boiled eggs, peeled and thinly sliced
4 tablespoons salad dress of choice.
  Rub garlic on a wooden salad bowl. Add the chickweed and eggs. Toss with the salad dressing. Serves 4.

---

90. CHICORY, *Chichorium intybus*
EDIBLE PARTS: Flowers, leaves and roots (Stems tough)
USES: <u>Flowers:</u> Raw; salads; teas; jellies; jams. Freeze in ice cubes or as popsicles. <u>Leaves:</u> Vegetable; raw; salads; teas. Cook in soups and stews; stir-fry. Dry for long term storage. <u>Roots:</u> Raw; salads; french-fry. Dry, grind as a coffee substitute. Dry or freeze for long term storage.

---

90. Chicory Coffee (or Dandelion Root)

1 teaspoon dandelion root or chicory root powder
1 cup water
  In medium saucepan, combine the powder and water. Bring to a boil and simmer, covered, for 3-4 minutes. Drink as coffee substitute. Serves 1.

---

91. ANNUAL SOWTHISTLE, *Sonchus oleraceus*
EDIBLE PARTS: All
USES: <u>Flowers:</u> Raw; salads; stir-fry; jellies; teas. <u>Leaves:</u> Vegetable; raw; salads; sandwiches. Cook in soups and stews. Dry or freeze for long term storage. <u>Roots:</u> Vegetable; raw. Cook in soups and stews; crockpot. Freeze for long term storage.

92. PERENNIAL SOWTHISTLE, *Sonchus arvensis*
EDIBLE PARTS: All
USES: <u>Flowers:</u> Raw; salads; stir-fry; jellies; teas. <u>Leaves:</u> Vegetable; raw; salads; sandwiches. Cook in soups and stews. Dry or freeze for long term storage. <u>Roots:</u> Vegetable; raw. Cook in soups and stews; crockpot. Freeze for long term storage.

91., 92., 95., 96. Vegetarian Burgers

2 cups cooked lentils
1/2 onion, peeled
2 tablespoons sow thistle leaves
  Steam and chop thistle leaves. Add all ingredients and mix until everything sticks together. Fry on each side until well done and browned. Makes 6 medium size burgers. (Freezes well.)

---

93. STINGING NETTLE, *Urtica dioica*
CAUTION: DO NOT COLLECT WITH BARE HANDS. WEAR GLOVES OR USE TONGS WHEN PICKING. ALL PARTS OF PLANT HAVE TINY STINGING HAIRS, WHICH CAN CAUSE PAIN, DERMATITIS, REDNESS, AND BLISTERS WHEN TOUCHED. COOKING DESTROYS HAIRS IMMEDIATELY. ALWAYS COOK NETTLES.
EDIBLE PARTS: All
USES: <u>Whole plant:</u> Vegetable; Cook in soups and stews; stir-fry. Simmer until tender. Dry, store in glass. Freeze for long term storage.

---

93. Nettle-Felafel Burgers

1 cup cooked and finely chopped nettles
1/2 cup felafel mix (see box for recipe)
2 tablespoons olive or safflower oil
  Place the nettles in a medium bowl and add the felafel mix slowly. Mix thoroughly. Add slowly a bit of water until a clay-like mixture results. Pat the mixture into a 3-inch patty. Heat the oil in a medium frying pan and fry the burgers slowly until brown on both sides, about 6 minutes. Serves 2-3 as a main course.

---

94. CURLY DOCK, *Rumex crispus*
CAUTION: IDENTIFY THIS ONE VERY CAREFULLY. ON THE DESERT, THERE ARE POISONOUS LOOK ALIKES. STUDY THE SEEDS AND FOLLOW THE FORAGING RULES. ALL PARTS OF DOCK HAVE EXTREMELY HIGH CONTENT OF VITAMIN A. VITAMIN A STORES IN THE LIVER. EATING LARGE PLANT QUANTITIES ARE UNADVISABLE.
EDIBLE PARTS: Young leaves and seeds in small quantities
USES: <u>Young Leaves:</u> Vegetable; raw; salads; sandwiches. Cook in soups and stews; stir-fry. Dry for long term storage. <u>Seeds:</u> Add small quantities to salads. Cook in soups and stews. Dry, store in glass for long term storage.

---

94. Curly Dock

HINTS: The entire plant can be used as excellent yellow dye. Seeds make a decorative craft material and are useful in flower arranging.

---

95. WHEELSCALE SALTBUSH *Atriplex elegans* (Left)

96. WRIGHT SALTBUSH *Atriplex wrightii* (Right)
CAUTION: ALL PLANT PARTS HAVE A SALTY TASTE. COOK IN SEVERAL CHANGES OF WATER. USE SPARINGLY IN OTHER DISHES TO REPLACE SALT. SALTBUSH MAY HAVE TOXIC LEVELS OF SELENIUM WHEN GROWN IN SELENIUM SOIL.
EDIBLE PARTS: Leaves and seeds

-13-

78

USES: Leaves: Vegetable. Cook older leaves. Young shoots may be eaten raw. Add as a salt substitute to meats and fish dishes. Dry for long term storage. Seeds: Grind to a powder. Use as a salt substitute.

Salt Bush Seasoning

Whole plant is salty. Native Americans use a 2" to 3" piece in a pot of soup for flavoring. Use ground seeds for salty flavor in soups, burgers and gravies.

---

97. MILK THISTLE, *Silybum marianum*
CAUTION: WATCH OUT FOR PRICKLES ON TIPS OF LEAVES. CUT OFF OR COOK TO DISSOLVE.
EDIBLE PARTS: Young leaves, purple fluff in seed head and seeds.
USES: Young leaves: Boil until prickles dissolve, or cut off prickles with scizzors. Vegetable; raw; salads; teas. Cook in soups and stews, crockpot. Dry or freeze for long term storage. Purple fluff and seeds: Remove with fingers or tweezers. Raw; salads; teas. Freeze in ice cubes or as popsicles. Dry, store in glass for long term storage.

---

97. Milk Thistle Soup with Yellow Squash

6-8 young milk thistle leaves
1 cup cooked, washed yellow squash
Place milk thistle leaves in water and simmer until soft and pliable (5-10 minutes). Puree in a blender. Place milk thistle puree and squash puree in two separate pots and heat. Pour the two purees simultaneously into a shallow soup bowl. Serve hot! (Optional, press garlic bud and sprinkle over the top.) Makes 1 cup.

---

98. LONDON ROCKET (Smooth leaves, 1 1/2-2 ft. tall), *Sisymbrium irio*

99. TUMBLE MUSTARD (Coarse leaves, 2-5 ft. tall), *Sisymbrium altissimum*

100. WILD MUSTARD (Broad radish like), *Brassica kaber*
CAUTION: EAT SPARINGLY FROM THE WESTERN VARIETIES. EASTERN STATES MUSTARDS ARE COOKED AS A POT-HERB IN QUANTITIES.
EDIBLE PARTS: All (small amounts only)
USES: Leaves: Vegetable; raw. One small leaf in a whole salad. Dry for long term storage. Flowers: Vegetable; salads. Small quantities raw on the trail. Freeze in ice cubes for long term storage.

101. BLACK MUSTARD (Fuzzy leaves), *Brassica nigra*

---

98. to 101. Stir-Fried Mustard Flowers

1 quart mustard flower heads
1 garlic clove, chopped
1 tablespoon olive oil
In a frying pan or wok, quickly stir-fry all ingredients over high heat until limp, about 2-3 minutes. Serve hot. Serves 4 as a side dish.

---

102. NODDING ONION, *Allium cernum*
EDIBLE PARTS: All
USES: Whole Plant: Use as an onion. Raw; boil; bake. All parts for a flavor additive. Dry or freeze for long term storage.

---

102. Nodding Onion Gravy

Use as onion in any recipe.
Wash and chop 2 cups of Nodding Onion. Put in 1-quart saucepan and cover with water. Simmer until tender, about 10 minutes. Season with Saltbush powder and peppergrass to taste. Blend in food processor until smooth gravy forms. Serve over potatoes or toasted Amaranth bread.

-14-

79

List of Grasses

A unique feature of the wild food walk is its extensive collection of grasses which we have listed below. These grasses are available for your identification. Please read the RED signs in each grass square for your own safety.

ANNUAL BLUEGRASS	*Poa annua*	5
ARIZONA PANICUM	*Panicum arizonicum*	53
BARNYARDGRASS	*Echinochloa crus-galli*	51
BERMUDAGRASS	*Cynodon dactylon*	56
BRISTLY FOXTAIL	*Setaria vertidillata*	40
BROWNTOP PANICUM	*Panicum fasciculatum*	55
CALIFORNIA BROMEGRASS	*Bromus carinatus*	44
CEREAL RYE	*Secale cereale*	59
CHEAT	*Bromus secalinus*	63
FALL PANICUM	*Panicum dichotomiflorum*	50
GOOSEGRASS	*Eleusine indica*	49
GREEN FOXTAIL	*Setaria viridis*	7
HARE BARLEY	*Hordeum leporinum*	2
ITALIAN RYEGRASS	*Lolium multiflorum*	6
JUNGLERICE-WATERGRASS	*Echinochloa colona*	38
LARGE HAIRY CRABGRASS	*Digitaria sanguinalis*	41
LEMONGRASS	*Andropogon schoenanthus*	57
LITTLESEED CANARYGRASS	*Phalaris minor*	58
MEDITERRANEANGRASS	*Schismus barbatus*	52
ORCHARDGRASS	*Daclylis glomerata*	64
PANICGRASS, Sangui Guarjio	*Panicum sonorum*	46
PURPLE NUTSEDGE	*Cyperus rotundus*	1
QUACKGRASS	*Elytrigia repens*	3
RATTAIL FESCUE	*Vulpia myuros*	43
SIDEOATS GRAMA	*Bouteloua curtipendula*	54
SMOOTH CRABGRASS	*Digitaria ischaemum*	42
SOFT BROMEGRASS	*Bromus mollis*	4
SOUTHWESTERN CUPGRASS	*Eriochloa gracilis*	60
SPIDERGRASS	*Aristida ternites*	61
UMBRELLAGRASS	*Cyprus altermifolius*	45
WILD OAT	*Arvena fatua*	48
WITCHGRASS-TUMBLE PANIC	*Panicum capillare*	39
YELLOW NUTSEDGE	*Cyperus esculentus*	62
YELLOW FOXTAIL	*Setaria glauca*	47

Grasses are used for FOOD, both as a FLOUR and as a SURVIVAL FOOD. Teas; broths. Cook in soups and stews. Use food blenders, processors, grinders in home use. GRASSES MAKE NUTRITIOUS FLOURS IN EVERYDAY BAKING.

CAUTION: PLEASE DO NOT EAT ANY GRASSES WITH BLACK DOTS,BLACK SEED HEADS, OR RED STEMS. BLACK MAY INDICATE MOLDS, SUCH AS DEADLY ERGOT. MOISTURE IS SOMETIMES TRAPPED IN SEED AREAS, CAUSING A BLACK FILM OF MOLD. THIS IS VERY EVIDENT. INSPECT THE GRASS PLANT CAREFULLY BEFORE EATING RAW FOR FOOD OR DRYING FOR FLOUR.

CAUTION: This wild edible plant walk is intended to be an educational tool for survival, as well as the home use of wild plants. The information presented here supplements a healthy, well-rounded life style. The nutritional requirements of the individual may vary greatly. Therefore, the consultants, City of Glendale, Glendale Public Library and the implementers take no responsibility for the individual use of ingesting wild plants.

Bring your notebooks, samples from your house for plant comparison. Start your own filing system from season to season. Experiment slowly.

Credits:
Wild Food Consultant and Tour Director, Linda Runyon
Xeriscape Consultant, David Schultz
Contributing Consultants: Richard & Stephanie Bond
Consultant, James Duke, Ph.D. Herbal Vineyard, Maryland
Wild Plants, Mike Morearty
Plant Drawings by Linda Runyon, taken from *National Field Guide From Crabgrass Muffins to Pine Needle Tea*, to be published.
Puffy Pete and Cuddles by Joan Schultz

Bibliography:
Library: Look under: Wild Plants, Natural Cookery, Vegetarianism, Survival, Native Plants, Native American Cooking.

GLENDALE

Glendale Public Library
5959 West Brown Street
Glendale, Arizona 85302

81

By the months of September, October and November, the plants were mature and had worked themselves full circle. The temperature at night was now 50 degrees. In November I knew the walk would be terminated by December. Had the walk been open the next year, we would have seen large areas of plants come up from seeds in a completely natural way. But we had the one year of our wild food exhibit at the public library of Glendale. The squares were planted with ornamental flowers, as had been seen before we cleared the squares out for our wild food walk.

Seeds from the following plants were gathered from the Glendale Walk in 1997 and used for germination in the New Jersey Walk years and years later: Burdock, broadleaf plantain, narrow leaf plantain, orchard grass, tumbleweed. The following seeds were saved from 1995 to 1999. The asterisked ones were still viable when grown in 2010.

burdock	shepherd's purse
plantain	dandelion
chicory	Queen Anne's lace
aster	milk thistle*
purslane	lamb's quarters*
curly dock	mints
malva neglecta	chamomile
clovers, red and white	thistle*
spearmint	mustard
sorrel*	primrose
amaranth*	chickweed
nettles	tumbleweed*

I learned a great deal about setting up a big walk that required help from a number of people, and made sure that I documented this one so that I would have the data learned for future walks. The next walk I did was much smaller, but very different, and it also was a valuable experience in its own way.

Tumbleweed Elementary School, 1998
Phoenix, AZ

A number of schools near the Glendale area requested that I share my wild food data with their students. David Schultz suggested that I accept one, and since all of my students knew about the Tumbleweed Elementary School, I accepted that request to work with their fifth grade class.

There was little concern in the early 90's about the nutrition of wild foods. The question came up in the fifth grade classroom where I was presenting the wild food materials, so I had a chance to go over all the species and how nutritious they were as a supplement to the students' diets. Quickly, the students picked amaranth and lamb's quarters as their top vegetables. Malva, prickly pear and sow thistle weren't far behind.

The top plants in nutrition became the starter plants, and were easily dug from areas around the school. Those plants were put in pots and set up by a door that was near the back porch of the classroom. The transplanted plants soon perked up and grew easily for all to see. During the two weeks that the root systems were getting stronger, the students and I together created the landscape plan that we followed for planting the potted plants into our designated walk space.

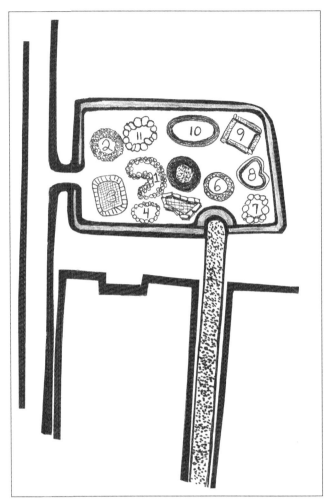

Tumbleweed Walk diagram.

The wild plants in this walk were:

1. wild lettuce
2. prickly pear
3. tumbleweed
4. desert plantain
5. cholla
6. milk thistle
7. malva

8. lambs quarters
9. amaranth
10. sow thistle
11. rosemary

12. aloe vera (not on the map, but was on school property near the walkway)

I used various edgings such as boards, small rocks, bricks, wire, large rocks, gravel. The central circle was around a Jacaranda tree.

Our chart for the students was started with the watering. Twice a day the nearby hose was put on mild, steady stream of water. The instruction was to carefully water the base of the plants by counting to 15 slowly. This became the second very important work column on the wall chart. Of course, items and instructions may vary with location, time of year, choice, and amount of area used for the walk.

Temperatures ranged from 80 degrees to 100 degrees before the two weeks were finished, and hats and suntan lotion were a must. Then the planting began. Working in teams, the students were so happy to be outside under the trees, digging holes after the hose had sprinkled all night. Mud was everywhere: shoes, hands, shovels, etc. The whole adventure was so much fun for 30 students and me. The teacher of the class came to inspect every hour or so.

No surprise that the one tree that overhung most of the land by the school building was a Jacaranda tree. I was already familiar with it from my Glendale Walk and the problems we had there. Big pods, almost like wood, 3-4 inches long, dropped with abandon any time, many times, and beaned almost every one of us as the days went on. For safety's sake, we were all schooled to not look up, and that hats and gloves were a must.

So, our work chart, in addition to showing what got watered when, included a column for picking up the Jacaranda pods. This was not as simple as you might imagine. Counting your pick-up total of Jacaranda buds for the day became a fun game to note on the chart. The total of one week was 408 of the darn things.

Gloves had to be used to help protect from the natural Arizona hazard that is the scorpion, big spiders, and black widows. Children are taught never to pick up anything from the ground without either turning it over with a stick first, or using gloves. One time the discovery of a scorpion led to a glass jar, and a classroom exhibit for learning purposes.

I always enjoy teaching children about wild food because I know how important it is for them to realize at an early age that they need not ever fear hunger.

PART 6: Back to the East Coast

A Natural Garden Walk, 2000-2008

Bridgeton, NJ

I moved back to the East Coast and in 2000, on my New Jersey farm, I put in an identification walk that lasted to 2008.

A New Jersey Wild Garden Walk.

The initial wood layout for the wild food plants.

Here is the "bare bones"—the beginning! This is the time to see what is coming up and then surround it for separation. This is undoubtedly the easiest way to "build" a wild walk. Just look, identify, and surround.

An identification garden may be grown in a line of plants, or, separating individual plants within a field is equally easily done. We used shingles for the separators because they were available and they did the job quickly. As the plants were not eaten but were only seen for identification, it was OK for a summer. Toxic

88

chemicals are used in the manufacturing of shingles and should not be used in an edible garden. When you want your walk to be edible as well as fulfill identification purposes, the black paper mentioned earlier is a better separator for the plants. Pebbles can be used but you still will need thick layers of black paper in between, and even that does not prevent the plants from creeping through eventually. I did learn that no growth is ever seen through or around shingles. They lasted easily for years and years.

The application of old shingles used to completely keep plant growth under control.

89

Around the perimeters and separate from the shingled identification area were field plants that I used for classes (which included grass classes), and from which I harvested for my own winter's larder.

Clover everywhere! Picking a stir fry

All grasses were picked in clean field areas
surrounding my old farm.

Fordville Walk, 2004-2005

Fordville, NJ

1st Year. Very elaborate, this 75-foot long walk took several truckloads of wood (4x4s and 2x2s) plus loads of mulch to complete. The total cost of supplies was around $200.00. The 2x2 sections had spill-over of individual plants because the New Jersey farm soil is so fertile and lush (weeds love it), that it caused this wild food walk to become difficult to maintain.

Because I was by myself now and did not have the additional help that would have allowed the walk to be properly maintained for visitors to easily identify the individual plants, it became a bit too overwhelming. I found that I had to let it revert back to nature after the first year, which was a shame because a lot of work went into its creation. However, I did keep records and the beautiful photos of growth which are shown in this book. The mullein grew 7-8 foot tall, for example, and the Queen Anne's lace flowers were saucer size. Given a crew of people, such as scouts, or nature park people who could properly keep up this level of wild food exhibit, such a wild food identification center would see literally thousands of interested people.

2nd Year. When I visited this walk, I noted most all the plants grew back in their individual plots, then spread out to take their place in the field.

3rd Year. By this time I was unable to find the separate exhibit plots at all. The plants were incorporated back into the original field, and someone must have moved the trees (probably by tractor) because none of the ones that were part of the walk did I observe.

The Fordville field before the walk.

The Fordville Walk in its glory.

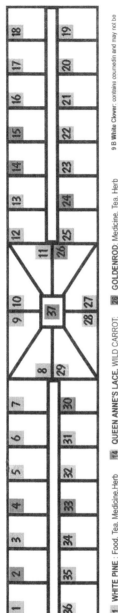

2004 Wild Food Walk Guide
at Fordville Crossing

1 WHITE PINE ; Food, Tea, Medicine, Herb
2 ALOE VERA; Medicine, Herb
3 AMARANTH; Food, Flour
4 BURDOCK; Food, Medicine, Herb
5 A. GERMAN CHAMOMILE, LEFT
5 B. ROMAN CHAMOMILE, RIGHT
   CHAMOMILE: Food, Tea, Medicine, Herb
6 CHICKWEED; Food, Herb
7 CHICORY; Food, Medicine, Herb
8 MULLEIN; Medicine, Tea, Herb
9 CLOVER; Food, Flour, Medicine, Herb
9 A. RED CLOVER, LEFT
9 B. WHITE CLOVER, RIGHT
10 PLANTAIN; Food, Medicine, Herb
10 A. BROAD LEAF PLANTAIN, LEFT
10 B. LONG LEAF PLANTAIN, RIGHT
11 DANDELION; Food, Flour, Herb
12 CATTAIL; Food, Flour
13 PRIMROSE, EVENING; Food, Medicine, Oil, Herb
14 QUEEN ANNE'S LACE, WILD CARROT; Food (Cautions apply)
15 A. PURSLANE; Food, Pickles
15 B. CURLYDOCK; Food, Herb
16 WILD PEPPER; Food, Spice
17 SORRELS; Food, Spice, Herb
17 A. FIELD SORREL
17 B. GARDEN SORREL
18 WILD LETTUCE; Food
18 A. PRICKLY WILD LETTUCE
18 B. BLUE LETTUCE
19 SASSAFRAS
20 MAPLE TREE, Seeds, Sap; Food
21 A. NUTSEDGE GRASS; Food, Flour
21 B. DRIED FOXTAIL GRASS
22 A. WILD OAT GRASS, Food, Flour
22 B. DRIED BARLEY GRASS
23 A. CRABGRASS, Food, Flour
23 B. DRIED CHEAT
24 YARROW; Medicine, Herb
25 THISTLE; Food, Herb
25 A. FIELD THISTLE, LEFT
26 B. BULL THISTLE, RIGHT

26 GOLDENROD; Medicine, Tea, Herb
26 A. FIELD GOLDENROD
26 B. ORNAMENTAL GOLDENROD
27 VIOLETS; Food, Herb
28 DAYLILY; Food
29 SUNFLOWERS, Seeds, Pith; Food
30 NETTLES; Food, Medicine, Tea, Herb, CAUTION: DO NOT TOUCH PLANT, Stinging hairs, Cook first before eating
31 MUSTARD; Food, Herb
32 MINTS; Food, Medicine, Tea, Herb
32 A. SPEARMINT, RIGHT
32 B. PEPPERMINT, LEFT
33 MILKWEED; Pods, Flower, Food, Med.
34 MALVA NEGLECTA; Food, Flour, Herb
35 LAMBS QUARTERS; Food, Flour
36 DAISYS; PETALS, LEAVES; Food
36 A. FIELD DAISY, RIGHT
36 B. SHASTA DAISY, LEFT
37 WILLOW TREE; Medicine, Herb (Found in Center)

GREEN CODED PLANTS are the most common vegetables. All parts are edible. Start consuming small amount, no more than 1/2 cup at first.
YELLOW CODED PLANTS have a caution attached.
5 A & B: Chamomile is a mild tranquilizer.

9 B White Clover: contains coumedin and may not be eaten by those taking blood thinners
17 A & B Sorrels: have to be cooked slightly, first to remove oxalic acid crystals, only a couple raw, please, consume in small quantities a day
19 Sassafras Tree: as a tea only, consume in small quantities a day
28 Day Lilies: may be cathartic in large quantities, only I or 2 to start.
29 Sunflower: have only edible seeds and stem pith.
30 A & B: Come to a survival class to learn how to EAT RAW PRICKLY THISTLE!!

RED CODED PLANTS
2 Aloe Vera: is a strong medicinal plant.
4 Burdock: lowers blood sugar, consume in only small quantities, please.
8 Mullein: may only be eaten in small quantities, as is a antihistamine.
14 Queen Anne's Lace: is entirely edible, all parts but look carefully and see the plants hairy stems this is your positive identification of a delicious "wild carrot" or Queen Anne's Lace it the stem is SMOOTH, BEWARE may be a look-alike-poison with white flowered top look carefully and please find the hairs before ingesting any part.
15 B Dock: is VERY high in vitamin A, so small quantities only.
24 Yarrow: is a stimulant and diuretic, consume small quantities or make tea.
26 Goldenrod: is also a blood tonic, eat sparingly, make tea, use tongs and dip in boiling water to destroy the hairs for safe eating.
37 Willow: is acetasclic acic, or aspirin derivative, eat under 6 inches is a medicine

We hope you enjoyed taking the "Wild Food Walk". My advice is to pick one or two plants and use them as your new vegetable! This will allow you to sample 2 varieties of plants then decide if you wish to sample others. The plants in this walk are found throughout the United States and other countries throughout the world. An abundance of free food awaits us all! Look down and eat up!

The handout we gave to visitors so they could identify the various plants in the walk.

Holding Tank for the Fordville Walk

Our walk here did not have a hose until long after the mature plants were planted. Why do I always have to do things the hard way? I knew I would need a reliable water source! What I had to do to get started was to collect five 5-gallon containers and a garbage can that I marked with a fill line a foot from the top. The reason for the line was because any more than that and the slopping and slurping of water easily flew out of the garbage can into my car. Every day in the heat I drove from my house to the walk area, and by hand with small 2 1/2 quart pails I watered the holding tank. When it rained, I was just so, so grateful.

Five gallon water containers took care of this holding tank.

Holding tank pots for this walk. Note the gravel in the cattail pot.

Most plants used about 5 gallon water containers every 3 days, and in between it rained, so we got a
break. Midway throughout the weeks of preparation a
house within a short distance became my water source.
I am so grateful to the couple that came over and asked
if I wanted to use their hose outside the house. I filled
my containers there for a month before I was able to
make an arrangement with a restaurant nearby to get
water directly, using a 400-foot hose that we ran from
their well to our site.

Hint: When you know it is time to move the plant
containers to their walk site for planting, do not water
them for a couple of days. It not only is easier, but they
will take in the water that is in the ground area when
planted. Some plants still wilt, others stand bold upright
overnight. Be patient with others, they will look absolutely dead and will come back up after a few days, or

95

grow new leaves from the soil next to the older stem. Remember, most wild foods are weeds. This toughness is very handy in a gardening exhibit.

The Fordville field was carefully marked with wood steaks. Below left shows the pile of 4x4s delivered. There was an initial order of 2 packs of 4x4s. A few extra had to be added in the end, but we were off and ready to build a walk for the public.

Staked-out Fordville field.

First load of 4 x 4s delivered to the site.

Next was figuring out the separators for the plants, such as the heavy black paper mentioned previously. I can tell you that these days there is a new fabric-like black cloth that works even better and this allows your plants to be safely consumed after harvesting.

Without my Mexican friends who understood my plants so well, this walk would have never come to fruition. The day we began, the temperature in New Jersey rose to 80 degrees. Several packs of 4x4s were laid in level sections of earth. All the plants that surrounded the pile in a wild state were the same plants as the walk itself. Bare ground in any state and country fills in with the "wild" weeds. It was so amazing to see the same plants in their natural state while taking this particular walk. The walk had the same plants growing up to maturity, while the surrounding field was mowed and grew new tiny plants all the time that could be easily compared to the exhibit of larger mature plants.

Getting ready to lay out the walk.

Laying out the 4 x 4's and leveling out dirt and wood for planting.

Planting aloes.

My friend Judy is planting her very own aloe in the exhibit. This very large mother plant gave us dozens and dozens of pups, or seedlings.

98

Aloe vera in the foreground, amaranth in the back.

I started making the exhibits alphabetical, but in the end, some beds did change for many reasons. I always planted smack in the middle of the exhibit space and most of the plants filled in quickly. Those that made only a central exhibit were beautiful though.

Barley grass (not seasonal at the time of the walk, so we used last year's dried samples.)

Foxtail and nutgrass (seasonal grass)

Burdock

Early burdock does not have the stalk with burrs. It takes two years for the stalk with burrs to grow. I only

100

put 4 plants in the exhibit, thank goodness. They became so large we had to remove 2 of them before the first year was out. I remember the 2 or 3 leaves on the seedlings came out of a pot that was medium in size. The roots were entirely root bound in that pot!

Mature prickly lettuce

Early prickly lettuce

You only need one plant to show how large and gorgeous prickly lettuce is. Upon maturity the top flowers were cut off by many students and used for food (as in stir-fries). The frequent harvesting of the flowers caused the plant to grow double flowers, which of course produced even more food. As we cut back on the leaves, the plants bushed out and became taller, and produced more seeds. We had 4 prickly lettuce plants and eventually had to remove 2 of them to keep that exhibit from being too dense. One plant grew to be 4-5 feet high. The leaves of prickly lettuce can also be used in stir-fries. The barbs, which are gelatin, dissolve and disappear readily when heated and cooked.

For months many meals were harvested from the blue lettuce plant (below). As you harvest wild lettuce, any specie, you will see the tiny replacement leaves coming from the joints left. After 8 feet was reached by the plant, we staked the plant on both sides, stringing with soft, green floral tape. Note: This tape will become your necessary tool during identification walks.

Blue lettuce

A very prolific plant, with yarrow it was so easy to just put a few plugs (young seedlings) here and there in the exhibit. Allow 6 inches between young plugs. Flowering will be evident in 2 or 3 weeks, and the bed of yarrow will became a solid mass with flowers in a very short time because yarrow spreads quickly.

Early yarrow

Flowering yarrow

I bought 4 rolls of 100 feet of black paper. Now we were really ready to start. We rolled the black paper out from each end to the circle in the middle. Then, we matched up the one roll with the other on the left. Over the middle circle, we did the same thing on the other side and didn't have but a couple of yards left. The center area was reinforced with the leftovers, then on to working out the water problem. •

Ah yes, the water problem. Five gallons of water were put on each exhibit whenever possible, but sometimes only a couple of gallons were poured on each plant. I usually put more on the plants that had a lot of seedlings, like a mint bed, or yarrow bed. They seemed to need more. Nettles also require more water, but aloe requires less.

Here I am, watering the exhibit plants by hand. I hauled water in 5 gallon containers for many weeks until the water hose was activated.

400 feet of hose from water source to plant exhibits.

Daily watering is so much easier!

Daily water became fun immediately! For all the volunteers also! The restaurant's well finally yielded water and the hose became my third arm. It did take 400 feet of new hose to go from the well to the site. (Another consideration one should plan on from the beginning.) From time to time, the prime went and we had to revert back to the containers again. I had made a mistake not figuring on this problem ahead of time. Water should always be available for a public walk!

When the truckloads of black mulch arrived, the fun began. We all got shovels and dug in the fresh pile of black mulch until there was 6 inches of mulch in the entire pathway, throughout the circle, and on the other side. I had to get another delivery of 4 yards of mulch by dump truck in between to finish. The whole process took 4 people 1 full day. Another truckload was delivered the following day, which was the mulch for around the plants. We knew the mulch would not stop the weeds entirely, but there were a few surprises over the summer.

The mulch pile.

Brandon wheeling a load of mulch.

For our cattail exhibit, we set it up similar to the one we did for the Glendale Walk, except that we put very heavy stones in the bottom of the container, put the cattail stems in, and then filled it up with loose gravel instead of sand.

Cattails

Amaranth

Six small amaranth seedlings grew into over 60 meals and crowded the exhibit. I would now recommend only two seedlings. We had to remove two of the six eventually so people could walk around the area. Several students used the exhibits for food and home cooked meals. I always encouraged that. In the field surrounding the walk you saw the giant amaranth plants mature higher than the other plants. There was enough food for hundreds of people in that field.

Short leaf and long leaf plantain

The short leaf plantain exhibit was planted just using a spoon. Soon, the lush growth was apparent.

I put long leaf plantain in the back of their exhibit and the short leaf in the front. Looked better that way! Also, when the plants go to seed, the difference between the long and short seeds are startling. One seed was the main reason we all needed to mow the lawn. If I had only known the seeds were the same as the health food stores! (I had even bought them in my younger, uninformed days.)

Dandelion

We all know dandelion and none of us could believe this exhibit did not thrive. It did not! Why, I have no idea. The 4 original plants matured, and stayed the same size for weeks. They never matured enough to spread. No flowers matured all summer. Red stems never appeared until early fall, which usually happens. The few plants remained green with some growth but almost no attempts to flower or become a lush exhibit. How ironic!

My favorite dandelion drawing

Purslane with aloe

As the tiny new seedling grew, the mat of purslane leaves began to form. Eventually we had to move the aloe plant to the rear of its exhibit because the tendrils grew out over into the walk mulch. Easy to move using a trowel, and nothing was disturbed.

As the purslane mat grew, the pinkish stems turned emerald green. One caution with eating as much wild food as you want is: <u>Watch out for red stems</u>. They become pink first and then red. The red stems means the plant has pulled up nitrates and that's what causes the red stems. Do not eat red stems!

Many flowers kept us busy picking them every day, and various plants were also picked regularly to give us more growth over the months. Plants must come to maturity in order to keep producing their seeds for many weeks.

Without this young man the walk would not have been possible. Kudos!

There are approximately 2 gallons of flour in the load of lamb's quarters Brandon is carrying. This load is completely lush lamb's quarters, one of the highest in nutrition of all the "weeds". The plant cuttings will be dried and ground to flour. I find hanging smaller handfuls to be the best way to dry large plant cuttings. If you can swish the plants so the air moves between the leaves easily, it will be dried properly. The amount you see in Brandon's harvest would be too thick to dry properly

111

and may rot some of the leaves that stuck together. I broke down these bundles into managable sections and draped them over a clothes line in the shade.

When I determined the leaves to be crackly and the stems would snap, they were ready to pull down onto the white sheet we placed under the clothes line. You can just swish the leaves off the stems easily, gather them in the sheet, and later convert the crinkly, dry leaves into powder or flour in a food processor, for instance, to use for food. The stronger stems can be turned into powder in a strong grinder. Storage data and recipes for the flour can be found in *The Essential Wild Food Survival Guide.* A little powder or flour goes a long way with this nutritious plant!

A typical class to taste test the sample plants after a wild food identification walk.

We had a learning room with this Fordville exhibit, and here's what it looked like.

Inside our Fordville Learning Room.

The shelves held common lawn teas (such as pine, spearmint, nettle, thistle, sassafras, sweet grass, rose, pansy, violet, mullein), and the tables held flour, leaves to be ground to flour, ect. I was so fortunate to be able to put tacks on the walls with all sorts of visuals, roots, ect. While an outside walk is of course highly desirable, I discovered that an indoor space where I could also show my stores of wild foods, and in some places even be able to give talks and show photographs or slides, helped to add to the wild food experience and understanding of the public.

Below shows a shelf of wild food teas. The fact is, throughout my life with wild food I found that many wild plants could be used for tea and I always kept a supply of wild tea on hand, especially for during cold winters!

Wild food teas stored in the Learning Room.

Wild Teas used by Linda

<u>From these trees</u>:

balsam

pine needle

willow

sassafras

pine bark

<u>From these plants</u>:

mints

comfrey

blessed thistle

field thistle

lemon balm

meadowsweet

chicory

clover, red and white

<u>From these bushes</u>:

nettle

rose

goldenrod

sweet gayle

raspberry

blackberry

<u>From these grasses</u>:

lemon grass

sweet grass

crabgrasses

barnyard

"Mediterranean"

foxtail

bullrushes

barley

<u>From these flowers</u>:

roses

yarrow

chamomile

marigold

clover

violets

pansies

goldenrod

dandelion

rose hip

Fordville Walk Grasses

All grasses have a different taste, ranging from the nutty to the sweet crabgrass. All the tastes and grasses are palatable. Check your Field Guide sources for all sorts of information about harvesting and storing grasses, and recipes to use for all the plants. You must harvest the grasses often as they will overhang and crowd each other out. What fun! I made sure to keep them harvested as they go to seed and blow all around the exhibit easily. Foxtail especially can become unmanageable real quick. Only a few seed heads are necessary to show people what they look like and the rest I kept clipped. Students learning about grasses were finding any of the walks an easy place to study and to take samples. Do tell people to take samples.

Grasses gathered from the Fordville Walk.

Grasses braided into rope.

My friend's grandson tries to break a grass rope in half.

117

Foxtail grasses.

Foxtail has a lot of wonderful edible seeds. In the old homestead days I found patches of foxtail grasses so prolific that I just had to figure a way to harvest without taking the plant out by the roots.

An old pillowcase became the easiest tool for gathering seed heads. I would pop the head off and place in the case if the seeds did not come off easily. One will note the changes in color over the season of the foxtail heads, from bright green to a beige color. When the seeds fall out by tapping, that is the time to gather. Tapping a bunch of ripe seeds into the pillowcase leaves the whole hull and stem for next year. By late summer, early fall, the seeds can actually be shaken off the stem with ease into the pillowcase. I have retrieved 1-2 quarts in record time this way. I did redry them in a clean, dry fry pan, then stored in glass for years. But, the tiny rice did not last very long in our

118

family. One reason is because foxtail makes the best stir fry rice. It takes around 1/2 cup to make a nice additive to a stir fry.

Stripping seeds off mature dried foxtail—seeds slide off stems easily!

Dried and ready for grinding to flour. To store, leave whole & unground.

Close-up of nutsedge or nutgrass. When dried and ground to flour for baking, this is a delicacy. Even a tiny amount creates a fabulous muffin!

Foxtail sample in a bunch.

120

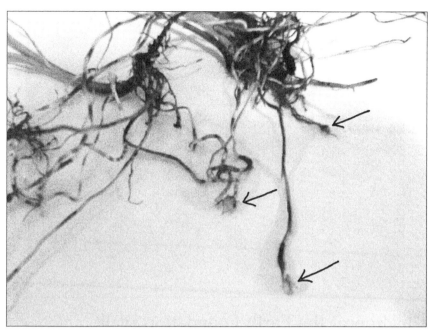

The arrows are pointing to the root corm, the nutlike bulb at the end of the roots -- a delicacy for the taste buds, and highly nutritious.

Soak dirt off grass harvest.

Children of the Earth Foundation Walk, 2004-2010

Greenwich, NJ

Children of The Earth Foundation (C.O.T.E.F.) is a non-profit school for children founded in Greenwich, New Jersey. I call this my "Potted Wild Food Plant Walk" because every wild plant in this walk was in its own pot. When the teaching season was over, I could simply pick up the pots and store them somewhere else for the winter, and then bring them back to the school every summer. If you don't have an area of land to rototill and plant for a walk, this is one way to go.

It was a beautiful spring day was when we made the first identification walk for COTEF school. Two wilderness instructors, Lisa Berry and Carleigh Fairchild, were from a school where I had taught and they came to assist me. Tools needed for this walk were: 2 shovels, 2 trowels, a bunch of black plastic pots, suntan lotion, bug repellant, sun hats, gloves, and a wheelbarrow or

122

wagon. Also needed were paper cards for labels and magic markers.

The entire walk of plants was placed in pots where they would be home for 7 years. As the plants remained in their pots all year round, maintenance was really a very simple matter. An additional benefit

COTEF Potted Walk diagram. From left to right: Sheep sorrel, sunflower, aloe vera, blueberry, yarrow, lamb's quarters, white clover, wild lettuce, wild rose, Queen Anne's lace, raspberry, mullein, amaranth, aster, violets, long leaf plantain.

My industrious helpers Lisa Berry and Carleigh Fairchild.

was that the water supply consisted of placing the pots in a semi circle by the hose area. So easy. New lush potting soil was added here and there, older plants removed, younger plants remained to grow to maturity, and so the walk shines again for another summer of education. Not to mention filling the empty spaces of young stomachs between lunch and dinner. Often the plants themselves were used for the main meals, or for sandwich filler. I can't count the amount of salads consumed from this semi-circle of wild food!

First Year: Plants were easily potted separately in native soil. The size of the pots varied to accommodate anticipated eventual growth. (Mullein grew to be 6 feet tall!) All plants were clipped and eaten from time to time, especially when a Wild Food Walk lecture was in progress. Children kept the plants watered.

Second Year: The pots were transported to my field for the winter, and were occasionally covered in snow.

<u>Third Year</u>: The plants were abundant, and even more dense than the first year. Seeds fell and the soil was full of each individual plant. The Walk was used by the school for another summer. The plants wintered with the owners of the school in southern New Jersey. In July, 2007, the plants have grown tall and quickly in the pots, just like the second year.

<u>Research Notes from the Third Year, 2007</u>: By the third year there was an abundance of:

red clover	violets
wild lettuce	dandelion
yarrow	spearmints
chicory	peppermints
nettles	

No sign yet (July) of lamb's quarters, amaranth, white clover, and all the others listed. Lamb's quarters and amaranth are the last to appear, usually August 1st or so, the hottest months. Milkweed, burdock, daisy, primrose, field sorrel were replanted. Usually, milkweed comes up every year from the existing roots. The other plants were easily replanted and grew prolifically.

By the end of August the amaranth and lambs quarters were 8" high. Dense amounts of purslane were found in existing pots, so it was easily transplanted to a single pot, as well as primrose. The wonderful thing about the potted walk is the ease in which you can obtain another plant and pop it out in the empty pot. They almost always grow fast.

<u>Research Notes from the Fourth Year, 2008</u>: This year, 2008, there has been little rain here. The Midwest has flooded extensively but on the east coast we have not

had rain to speak of. The pots were not watered most of the winter, and I am told the pots stayed out all winter as planned.

I first saw the plants again in the COTEF camp around the 1st week of June. There was extensive growth, even though the pots were stripped systematically by the children over the first week or so. We know the majority of the plants rejuvenate quickly. This is the plan for teaching the young ones to eat and enjoy—the plants regrow as fast as parents mow the lawn at home.

Clovers, mints, plantains, dandelions, rejuvenate especially quickly. I have been told the children can now identify and eat the common wild foods found in most dirt spots. We teach to not pick near a car path, to check the cards, to read the information if in doubt, and tell an adult if you see a strange plant. This is where good maintenance comes in and why I say that volunteers are treasured gifts to a wild food walk!

The most extensive growth was with these plants:

all mints	garden sorrel
clovers	aloe vera (kept indoors)
wild lettuce	chamomille
Queen Anne's lace	daisies
plantains	primrose

Following are some photographs from when I taught at the COTEF camp over the summers I was there.

126

127

Data I learned from this potted walk:

1. Nettles and mints take a lot of water. Water first, then go back and water them again.

2. Burdock only has burrs the second year. Just wait or pick a branch of old burrs, as we did, and push the end into the exhibit for the kids to see.

3. The weeping willow tree grows too big for the pot after the first year. We planted that one by the lake, and a new one was potted up each year. Easy to do, just push the bigger end of the willow stick into the ground! Water it well because it sprouts many roots and grows well.

4. The pine tree has slow growth over the years.

5. Pull out most of the mints, nettles, clover, plantain, anything that has excessive growth. Leave a few when they go dormant because they will spring up in spring!

132

6. The best way to introduce bark to anyone is by chewing a dried, crispy string of inner tree bark. Children are my greatest critics of the taste test! They always love this! Not too strong tasting, but stimulates the senses, and makes one realize some tree barks are edible. There is a quantity of data about edible trees and bark in my book *Eat the TREES!*

Survival Backpack Kit

As COTEF is a survival camp for children, I realized that helping them to know about the importance of a wild food backpack kit (which they can pack into their backpack they take with them for camping trips, traveling, etc.) was a good idea. I had already compiled data for such a kit for adults and knew that these children interested in wild food survival could also benefit from the information.

Next is the basic data for such a kit, but it can be changed according to one's needs to feel safe for a few weeks or months.

Wild Food Survival Backpack Kit

Wild Plant Food—Basic Six. Be sure that you are fully confident of your identification of each wild plant listed below, and review your data sources as to particular benefits of each item included in your kit. We sealed everything in ziplock sandwich bags which are cheap and light.

1. Amaranth Seeds: 1/4 of a bag of seeds winnowed from the tops of a dozen Amaranth plants or 1/4 bag of dried black seeds from your health food store.

2. Lamb's Quarters Leaves: 1/2 bag of pure lambs quarters powder or flour.

3. Red Clover Leaves and Heads: 1/2 bag of red clover flour; in a separate bag, two or three handfuls of dried whole heads.

4. Purslane: 1/4 bag of powdered plant mat flour (generally about 3 quarts of the gathered plant mat part will yield this much flour).

5. Plantain Leaves and Seeds: 1/4 bag of plantain leaves flour; in a separate bag, enough seeds to fill it 1/4 full.

6. Dock (Curly Dock) Leaves, Seeds, Roots: 1/4 bag flour (generally about 1 quart of leaves); in a separate bag; enough seeds in a separate bag to fill it 1/2 full; two or three roots, stripped and stored dry in bag.

Medicinal Plants. Check your wild food references on each of these plants so you feel comfortable including them in your kit.

Mullein: One fairly large mullein leaf (around a foot long) that has been dried thoroughly til it is crispy and

134

easy to crumble by hand (called "rough grinding"), and stored in its baggie. One such mullein leaf is enough for an emergency survival pack.

Eccinacea Root: This is not one of the 50 plants included in my Field Guide, but the benefits of having this plant in your kit is great, so I recommend that you include 1/2 baggie of dried root slivers (about the width of a shoe lace) in your kit.

Yarrow: dried flowers, stems and leaves, 1/2 bag total.

Marigold: 4 or 5 dried flowers, rough ground or crushed.

Thyme: Little leaves stripped off stems to add up to 1/4 baggie.

Cayenne Pepper: The whole pepper dried, or crushed into 1/8 bag. You can just store a few dried peppers, or pour some cayenne from your spice cabinet source. (Also not in my book, but very useful.)

Weeping Willow: A handful of 6" twigs in a baggie.

Kelp: Purchase this from your health food store, as it is not a wild plant but is also very helpful.

Pine Sap: The sap can be picked off a pine tree using a sharp stick. You can roll the sap in wax paper and then use a table knife to scrap the sap into a small hard plastic vial with a lid. It will crystalize in the vial into a firm candy-like substance that should keep for years. Add the vial to your kit.

Dried Blueberries: 15 - 20 dried berries in a baggie.

More Roots, Leaves, Tree Barks.

Burdock Roots and Dandelion Roots: Strip into shoelace size width, dry and store 1/2 bag.

Chicory Roots: Strip into shoelace size width, stripped and stored dry 1/2 bag.

Mint Leaves: Crumble from whole to rough grind to make 1/2 bag.

Pine Bark and Birch Bark: Store hunks to fill 3/4 bag.

Healthy Sweet Alternatives.

Wheat Sprout Flour: Powdered, 1/2 bag.

Stevia: Boxes of individual packets of this excellent and natural sweetener are available not only in health food stores but now you can probably find them in your regular grocery store as well.

Mesquite Beans: While these beans may not be local for many folks, I am including them here because they are very high in carbohydrates and amino acids, which additionally gives them a sweet taste and is like candy to me. If you want to include the mesquite bean in your kit, you should be able to find them for sale on the internet.

Meadowsweet Flowers: Crush enough to make 1/4 - 1/2 bag.

Rose Petals: Crush enough to make 1/4 - 1/2 bag.

PART 7: General Tips for Wild Food Walks

Additional Data on Seedlings

Creating a wild food walk from seedlings could be a big part of your preliminary actions for the walk. Here is more data for you on that subject.

Prepare the container for the seedlings. Potting soil is best. Align the soil type that has built-in moisture retaining beads and nutrients. Water the soil thoroughly and drain. Take a tablespoon and press in indentations spaced apart. Here are some examples for planting the seedlings of the following plants:

Lamb's Quarters:	3" deep, 12" apart
Amaranth:	3" deep, 12" apart
Curly dock:	2" deep, 6" apart
Chicory:	2" deep, 6" apart
Mustard:	1 1/2" deep, 4-5" apart
Dandelion:	1 1/2" deep, 4-5" apart
Plantain:	1 1/2" deep, 4-5" apart
Thistles:	3" deep, 6" apart

Use a tablespoon to scoop out to the depth indicated. Place the plug in the hole and tamp down the dirt around the main stem. When you finish, mark seedlings with a tongue blade, or some people use plastic spoons and permanent markers.

If the seedlings are in direct sun, you will need to water more often 2x's a day in 90 degrees as necessary. I use a sprinkling watering can or sprinkler end to a hose so the young seedlings are not injured. I water in the morning thoroughly and in evening for great root growth.

Starting seedlings.

Seedlings 3-4 weeks old. Upper row: dandelion, chicory.
Lower row: chamomile, curly dock.

The curly dock area in the photo shows a pink color. This pink color indicates the seedling, for some

138

reason, is pulling up nitrates from the potting soil. This is very unusual for young new plants not fully mature. I have no idea what might have caused this in the dock. In soil, the nitrates pull up after the plant is usually fully mature. I have seen young plants, seedlings, even small trees bright red at the base of a water stream that was coming down from an Adirondack mountain.

For the curly dock seedlings I removed the pink leaves and stirred up the soil, adding a bit more. The green, healthy leaves began to take over the area.

Young wild food plants.

Growing dandelion leaves will show serrations, saw-tooth edging, 4 leaves in pairs. Chickweed shows 4-6 leaves, 2-4 inch tendrils. With clover, the first tiny 3 leaves appear and unfold by the dozen in all areas of the plant. Curly dock has larger leaves, 4 or 6 leaves now, but no curl present as yet. Chamomile has a 1" long tall center spike in the center of each tiny leaf bunch. The taste is somewhat bitter until the branches flower. I do not shear the chamomile until it is more mature with flowers.

139

As to violets, be sure to only pick the large leaves for food. Also, these large violet leaves, and the large malva neglecta leaves too, make wonderful wrappers for fried beans and salsa!

Six week old violets.

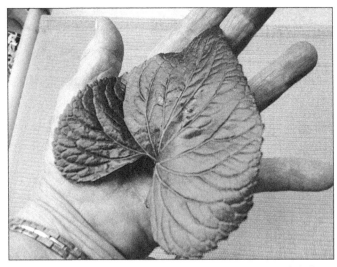
A large violet leaf. The larger leaves are the ones to pick for a wrap.

Chickweed.

A pot of salad greens. Sheared then dried, I label their stored jar "nutrient additive".

Plantain shoots with one lamb's quarters seedling growing in the middle.

Lamb's quarters.

This one lamb's quarters plant is equal to four large meals. When cut back drastically this plant will regrow in a week or so, over and over. What vegetable do you know that is this nutritious, this fast growing, and absolutely free?

Mint.

These mints grew rapidly. Many, many cuttings will yield bags of dried mints for storage. High in iron and tasting wonderful, mints make a tasty and healthy additive to any dried greens, and just in general.

Clover big enough to be sheared and added to salad.

143

Larger growth seedlings.

Whenever you grow plants, here are some things to be careful of: Watch the tips of leaves carefully, especially the green and fragile ones, i.e., lamb's quarters, amaranth, malva. If the tips begin to dry, curl, are not erect or look wavy, something is wrong. Usually a large dose of water will correct the plant, but if it doesn't, expect probably mites, red mites, or other insect problems. Examine carefully for these, as white flies or mites will show themselves through the tips of leaves first. Careful examination is imperative.

144

Before removing the seedling from its potted seed home, sprinkle the soil to make it damp for easier transfer to the ground. Note that the plants being moved to a new area might have become too big for your container. In the case of the plant having become bush-like, repot the seedlings into separate individual pots.

You should know that chicory sort of meshes together as the seedlings mature. I find it convenient to use these plants for salad or dried ingredients. Just shear with scissors every time the "lawn" looks like it needs to be cut.

Edible Plants and Meal Suggestions

This thistle is very fast growing. I cut individual leaves off for soup, or vegetable portions, or tea. One thistle can make up to 30 meals.

"Mother" thistle with several "pups", which can be repotted to become another 3 foot plant.

145

One summer I farmed 2 plants for the first 2 months of summer. As the plants got to maturity, they put up the pod top for the final seeds under the thistle fluff. The buds are edible, friable, and very delicious. I used the end buds once, and then several times after that. Cut off cleanly, another one will form. I waited two weeks and went back to find the new tops of thistles. These are very rapid growing plants. The roots of a thistle can be used for winter's storage, but the plant must go to maturity. Freezers can be filled with thistles for soups and vegetable stir-fries.

This single wild lettuce plant (below) grew next to my apartment and provided me over 50 salads, and vegetable dried leaves. I would just clip, and the joint would grow 3 or 6 more leaves. At the bottom, many "pups" (not unlike the picture of the thistle pups)

Wild lettuce plant outside my apartment.

replaced themselves and grew to 8 feet tall and provided me many more frozen and dried vegetable stores.

That wild lettuce plant started out as a potted seedling but it grew so big I had to harvest it to keep it from tipping over from the leaf weight. As I pulled the leaves down, the joint bled white milk, and this is the caustic, herb taste of this plant. The *Bible* refers to it as the "bitter herb of the field" several times.

As to how to cut that plant's prickly spine away from the large leaf, here's my method: Put the leaf face side down on a tray, prickles side up. Then fold the leaf in half with the prickles on top. Now you can easily shear them off with scissors. Then I cut the strips into 1-2" pieces and add them to my salad raw! I suggest that you start sparingly in eating this plant because wild lettuce, though highly nutritious, has a bigger leaf.

A sow thistle is more filmy, or fragile, than wild lettuce. A sample "twig" from a sow thistle is entirely edible.

Sow thistle.

147

My neighbor's organic flower garden became a wonderful area. I could help her weed plus supply myself with a winter's larder. She had so much sorrel I couldn't help but string up a stash of it. Steeped in water, sorrel will make French sorrel soup in just a few minutes. Here's how: To prepare for the soup, all one does is cut off the plant above the root structure. Then put that in a pot with water to cover. Swish around a lot, and strain the plant material. I run water again over the sieve a few times.

Don't forget, this shamrock leaf plant grows in all states and is a real pain to weed often here in the Northeast. But think of the nutritious soups in the winter!

"Ropes" of sorrel.

Dried sorrel, ready for storage.

148

Shown are feverfew flowers, lavender, and lamb's quarters from our harvest.

A colorful wild harvest.

Here's an artistic way to create a small garden walk that includes wild food.

A colorful wild harvest.

Facts to Know About Wild Food Walks

1. Prolonged rain will cause growth to slow or stop. A white mold will eventually form and wilt fragile leaves, i.e.; dandelion, clover, wild lettuces, sow thistle. More than 3 full days of rain may start this process. One day of sunshine will stop the process.

2. Milk-filled plants like milkweed and wild lettuce have stems that may yellow and harden when prolonged rain or excessive watering occurs. The process will not reverse, although healthy leaves and limbs from yellowed stems will flourish.

3. Milk thistle is the home for mounds of red ants. Use tongs to gather up leaves on or close to the ground. The ants will swarm and sting before you can remove your hand if you try to break off leaves naturally.

4. The most prolific growth is always the amaranth and milk-thistle in hot states or countries. The mints are always the most prolific in more average temperatures. Clover, daisies, mints, violets have the most prolific growth in the east. Malva, amaranth, tumbleweed daisies, and milk thistle are the most prolific in the desert states.

5. Pull out or shear with scissors the seed pods from sorrel. This will help keep exhibits more trimmed, and keep sorrel from spreading. Pull off seed spires from amaranth or lamb's quarters. This will cause the plant to branch out and go to seed at the end of each branch.

6. Sunflower bushes grow bushier by pulling off flowers on the ends, forming a more egg-shaped bush. The rest of the branches will go to seed faster and more blossoms will occur.

150

7. Red stems are nitrated specimens, whether east or west. Just remove the red stems and discard the whole plant. If there are seeds on the plant, remove, dry, and save before discarding the specimen. In some cases, I shear to a ground level, leaving about a foot.

8. Peacocks love primrose whorls. The peacocks were loose in one of my walks and we gave in and had to screen the samples. As soon as the center stem begins to rise over the screen level, we could remove them safely. Only the young seedlings were attractive to the birds. Deer and turtles will eat most anything. There are deterrents for both in your neighborhood farm, market, or hardware store.

9. Whether you rototill a swatch of dirt, dig an aerated garden square, or prepare an elaborate section of your backyard for a walk, let the freshly turned soil sit for a week or so before planting anything.

10. In time, stakes, and a way to tie the plant to it, are needed to support bushes, burdock, wild lettuces, Queen Anne's lace, milkweed, sunflowers, for instance. You can purchase green ties for this, or green-colored string can be used if not too thin, which would cut the stems.

11. If you have any hills or down-trending land, plant at the bottom of the incline. Plants need rain and moisture, and that's easier to accomplish downhill. A drip spout around a house may be the best place for a walk to be. Sorrel especially enjoys a drip area; nettles and mints also grow abundantly in moist areas. Another planning suggestion is to arrange to place many plants near your entrance driveway, so that when people are leaving your toured area, they will get another chance to see wild plants on their way back to their car.

12. Because the following plants are quite hard to grow, sometimes I transplanted a whole mature plant and let it dry, just to exhibit the plant for identification purposes: blueberry, raspberry, blackberry, maple tree, red sumac.

Suggested Actions for a Successful Walk

A. Once you know the land area for your walk, diagram your plant arrangement, including your edgings and accessories. Also determine where your water supply will come from, how you will set up a holding tank area if needed. etc. Research the wild plants that naturally grow in your area so you can include them, along with others of the wild plants that you want to display in your walk. Have a well thought out plan as your first action towards establishing a wild food walk.

A photo of basic wild food plants at my Glendale Walk.

B. If you are planning a substantial identification walk so people can learn about wild food survival, research the laws and guidelines in your area to be sure you will be in compliance with them. You don't want to devote a lot of time to planning and creating a wild food walk only to find out that zoning laws or something of the sort would prohibit you from keeping your walk open to visitors, or that you can't request a donation for it.

C. Consult with local Master Gardener clubs as well as nurseries in your area for data or items that might be useful to you.

D. Make sure that you have volunteers lined up to help you set up and plant the walk, and to keep it going. For a walk of any significant size, a group effort here is essential to success. A large exhibit such as the Glendale walk needs 3 or 4 volunteers for about 4-5 hours a day, 6 days a week. The amount of time can be cut in half by cutting the size of the walk in half.

E. Be prepared for outdoor work and dress accordingly. In a hot environment, always wear a hat, long-sleeve shirt, sunblock lotion. Wear gloves to protect your hands.

F. Study up on wild food in general, and your plants in particular so you can answer questions that will come up. If you are planning a hand-out sheet or brochure for your visitors, make sure that is ready well before your opening date. Also work out and do any promotional actions that could help you contact people who might be interested in learning wild food data.

G. Keep a complete chart of daily details for the walk clearly posted for easy reference. In addition to usual upkeep and maintenance, also include actions such as insect control or dealing with wild food predators.

H. Every day, prior to your public hours of operation, go around each exhibit and remove dead plants or plant parts, debris, litter, trash, garbage, eyesores, etc., anything that would take away from the best presentation of the exhibit. Have trash cans coveniently located throughout your walk so that you and your public have disposal places. As you go through the walk, check to make sure your identifying markers or signs are straight and easy to read. A nice presentation will encourage people who come to your wild food exhibit to recommend it to their friends and neighbors.

PART 8: Presenting Wild Food to the World

Once I understood that I had a responsibility to communicate to everybody the concept of "free wild food" far and wide, I searched for venues from which to spread my message. I really wanted other people to realize that they need never fear starvation at any time or for any reason, as long as there was dirt nearby. The wild food walks were one way to get the word out, plus I did presentations for various groups that were interested in learning what I had to say.

Those were very enjoyable experiences for me, to have people interested in my materials come see me personally, and so I would have them sign my guest book. I also encouraged them to check out my website to find out more about my wild food life adventures, and how to acquire valuable wild food survival data.

People interested in finding out about wild food at my display table.

A display table I set up that shows some of the wild food materials that we have created.

When I began teaching wild food survival, I was one of a very few number of people who had experience in living off the land through wild edible food. Since then, I am so happy to see that many others have taken it up and are spreading the word.

My friend Holly lives in the Appalachian Mountains in North Carolina. She has read all of my books and other materials to find out about the wild plants that grow so profusely in her back yard, and has become quite expert as a forager, storer and preparer of wild food. She is active in blogging about her wild food adventures and successes, and often teaches classes and does wild food presentations for such highly worthwhile organizations as Samaritan's Purse. I am pleased that I had some part in the wonderful work that Holly does, and it is my hope that thousands more the world over become willing to help bring food security to mankind.

156

My friend, Holly Drake, of WildBlessings.com at her "wild" display table.

People interested in Holly's items. She also had some of my books on the shelf just above and to the right.